*T*his book belongs to

_____

*a young woman
loved by God.*

A Young Woman's Walk with God

Elizabeth George

HARVEST HOUSE PUBLISHERS

EUGENE, OREGON

Cover design by Dugan Design Group, Bloomington, Minnesota

Cover photo © Kate Powers / Taxi / Getty Images

Italicized text in Scripture quotations indicate author emphasis.

Acknowledgment

As always, thank you to my dear husband, Jim George, M.Div., Th.M., for your able assistance, guidance, suggestions, and loving encouragement on this project.

A YOUNG WOMAN'S WALK WITH GOD
Copyright © 2006 by Elizabeth George
Published by Harvest House Publishers
Eugene, Oregon 97402
www.harvesthousepublishers.com

Library of Congress Cataloging-in-Publication Data

George, Elizabeth, 1944-
  A young woman's walk with God / Elizabeth George.
     p. cm.
  Includes bibliographical references (p.   ).
  ISBN 978-0-7369-1653-0 (pbk.)
  ISBN 978-0-7369-3198-4 (eBook)
  1. Teenage girls—Religious life.   2. Christian teenagers—Religious life.   I. Title.
  BV4551.3.G47 2006
  248.8'33—dc22   2005029083

Printed in the United States of America

12 13 14 15 16 / BP / 13 12 11 10 9

Contents

Getting Your Act Together

A Word of Welcome

Dear Friend,

Without even meeting you, I can tell you are someone very special! Why? Because you're choosing to read this book. When you consider its title, it becomes pretty obvious that you desire to love God with all your heart. This book is packed with information and how-to's that will show you how to fulfill the desire of your heart—how to grow more like Jesus! As we begin our journey together, a few things will make it even sweeter.

Open your book...and enjoy it! Everything you need is here. I've tried to make it convenient for you as a busy young woman. In my mind I've pictured you reading this book on your bed at home, in a bunk bed at camp, on your family vacation, in a lounge chair sunbathing around a pool, even in the library after you've finished your homework. Enjoy your book, carry it with you, and let God's Word instruct you.

Open your heart...to your friends. Encourage them to get books too. Then you will each be growing, which means your friendships will be growing in the right direction—in the things of the Lord. A godly woman needs other godly women as friends. So invite them to join you.

Open your heart...and look around. Are there any girls you don't know very well at school, or in the neighborhood, or perhaps where you work, who you can invite to join your study? Girls who need the Savior? Who need some guidelines for their lives? Who need a friend? Whisper a prayer to God, be bold, and reach out and· invite someone you'd like to know better to get together.

Open your heart...to the topics covered in this book. They are just what every gal needs. They'll give you God's wisdom and guidelines for your thoughts, words, and deeds...and for your walk with Him.

Open your heart...to the Holy Spirit through prayer. Ask Him to illuminate God's Word, to help you understand His plan for you to enjoy His presence in you. Let Him transform your life into something amazing.

Open your heart...and dream! Dream of the woman you yearn to be—a woman who walks with Jesus every day in every way.

It is the prayer of my heart that the contents of this special book will encourage you, excite you, instruct you, and inspire you to passionately follow in Jesus' steps!

In His great and amazing love,

Elizabeth George

1

Getting It All Going

I live in the state of Washington. And never in my life would I have dreamed it, but right in my front yard is an apple tree! That means I get to watch God's process for the miraculous production of apples from start to finish each year. But believe me, I know very well the work it takes me and my husband to do our part in improving and increasing a crop of apples! We nurture, fertilize, water, prune, train, spray, and protect this tree…and our efforts have definitely paid off.

As I think about our amazing apple tree, I can't help but wonder about the fruit of our lives as Christian women, no matter what our ages. Should you and I pay any less attention to our own fruitfulness—in our case the spiritual kind—than Jim and I do to an apple tree? Shouldn't we be actively cultivating the fruit of the Spirit in our lives so we reflect the glory of God and the beauty of Christ? But what exactly can we do to get the growing of spiritual fruit going? What practical steps can we take to get it all together so we become more like Jesus?

Finding Out About the Fruit of the Spirit

Well, just as I studied to learn more about my apple tree and the fruit it produces, you and I need to study God's Word to better understand the fruit of the Holy Spirit and how it grows. Take your favorite pen in hand now and interact with these truths from the Bible. And if it's not a good time—you know, you don't have a pen, you're on the bus, or you're getting ready to turn out the light and get some much-needed sleep—then just read along for now.

✎ *A Word from God's Word About Fruit...*

- The word "fruit" is used throughout the Bible to refer to telltale evidence of what is on the inside of a person. If what's inside is good, then the fruit of that person's life will be good. But if what's inside is rotten, the fruit of that person's life will be bad. That's what Jesus taught when He said,

  Make a tree good and its fruit will be good, or make a tree bad and its fruit will be bad, for a tree is recognized by its fruit....The good man brings good things out of the good stored up in him, and the evil man brings evil things out of the evil stored up in him (Matthew 12:33,35).

  What sort of fruit have you seen in your actions lately?

- Any person who has received Jesus as Savior and Lord and has Christ living within will bear good fruit. He will be *"filled with the fruit of righteousness that comes through Jesus Christ—to the glory and praise of God"* (Philippians 1:11). How do you think exhibiting the fruit of righteousness brings glory and praise to God? And in what ways has the fruit you are bearing shown others what Jesus is like?

- The fruit of the Spirit has been described as "those gracious habits which the Holy Spirit produces in the Christian."[1] In Galatians 5:22-23, the apostle Paul lists these "gracious habits"— *"the fruit of the Spirit is love, joy, peace, patience, kindness, goodness, faithfulness, gentleness and self-control."* All nine fruit stand together and make up our walk with God. They are like a string of Christmas lights— there is one string with many lights that all light up at once when plugged into the electrical socket. But if one bulb goes out, the entire string goes out. That's how God's fruit is borne in our lives. Not one of them can be missing, and all must be evident—lit up—to be God's fruit. As you recall your actions today, were any of these spiritual habits missing? What must you do to get "plugged into God," the power source, again?

"So What Can I Do?"

I'm sure you want God's fruit to mark your life, to make you beautiful from the inside out. If that's true, you probably wonder, "So what can I do? How can I make this happen? What do I need to do to get things going, to get this business of spiritual fruit-bearing in motion?"

Well, first, here's one thing you can't do. You can't think, *Perhaps if I just try harder...* No, Jesus teaches that do-it-yourself effort isn't the answer. The fruit of the Spirit can only be produced as we yield to God and allow His Spirit to work in us as we walk through the events and encounters life brings our way each day.

Next, remember that the fruit of the Spirit act as one. They are like a watch that contains many parts. A watch can be taken apart for cleaning and repair, but each piece must be put back into place for the watch to run. In this book, we will take apart and inspect each fruit of the Spirit. Then we'll see how they all work together to present a whole, just like a watch.

Here's another thing you can do: Realize that, as a whole, the nine characteristics of the fruit of the Spirit are all produced in the same way. Everything that is said of one characteristic is true of the other eight. They are one and the same fruit, interwoven and related to one another. And they are produced as we look to God.

Finally, never for a second forget about the battle that is going on between your flesh and the Spirit. In Galatians 5:17 we learn that "the sinful nature desires what is contrary to the Spirit, and the Spirit what is contrary to the sinful nature. They are in conflict with each other, so that you do not do what you want." You and I will face this struggle—the struggle between the flesh and the Spirit—until the day we die. But, praise God, when we walk or "live by the Spirit... [we] will not gratify the desires of the sinful nature" (verse 16). We will have victory over the flesh—our body and its cravings—when we walk by the Spirit.

So, what does it mean to walk by the Spirit? In simple terms, walking by the Spirit means:

> Living each minute God's way—obeying Him.
> Seeking to please God with...
> > the thoughts we choose to think,
> > the words we choose to say, and
> > the actions we choose to take.
>
> Letting God guide us each step of the way.
> Letting God work in us so we can bring glory
> > to Him.

Discovering the Secret to Walking with God

Are you catching on? Are you getting it? It is only as we walk by God's Spirit that we show forth Christ in our lives. And it is only as we "abide" in Christ that God gives us the grace to do this. This, my friend, is the secret to walking with God: We must abide in Christ. Jesus said in John 15:4-5:

> *Remain in me, and I will remain in you. No branch can bear fruit by itself; it must remain in the vine. Neither can you bear fruit unless you remain in me. I am the vine; you are the branches. If a man remains in me and I in*

> *him, he will bear much fruit; apart from me you*
> *can do nothing.*

What's the point? Only by abiding or remaining in Him can you and I as followers of Jesus bear fruit (verses 2,4,5). To "abide" or "remain" means

> "continued fellowship with the Lord,"[2]
> "dwelling in His fellowship and being submis-
>   sive to His will,"[3] and
> keeping "contact with Jesus...a constant con-
>   tact."[4]

Here's where our *doing* comes in. Like all I *do* to help my apple tree along, there are a few things you can *do* that help you abide in Christ. Let's call them "fruit boosters." These four practical steps—things you can *do*—will help you remain in constant contact with Jesus, to abide in Him, to remain close to Jesus and dwell in Him as He dwells in you.

   1. *Get into God's Word*—One Bible teacher explains, "Abiding cannot be maintained [without]...giving the words of Christ a...[reigning] position in the heart (cf. Colossians 3:16)."[5] So...be diligent about spending time in God's Word. Make it your habit to get into your Bible, to read it, study it, and meditate on it on a regular basis. Don't merely go through the motions. Instead, work at making your time in God's Word full and meaningful.

   2. *Make time for prayer*—Prayer is a must for walking with God. I read some time ago that "no blessing of the Christian life becomes continually possessed unless we are

men and women of regular, daily, unhurried, secret lingerings in prayer."[6]

Here's a question for you. Would others—your family and
friends, teachers and other students—describe you as a
person of "regular, daily, unhurried, secret lingerings in
prayer"? Do whatever you have to do to make prayer a vital
link between you and God. Through prayer you learn more
about God, His heart, and His purposes. To abide in Christ
and be a woman who walks with God, do all you can to
develop your prayer life. (And P.S., to learn more about
prayer, read my book *A Young Woman's Call to Prayer.*[7]
There's nothing you can't talk about with God!)

3. *Do what God asks*—Your waking prayer each morning
should be to make choices that honor God and His Word,
to really love God! Jesus said, "If you obey my commands,
you will remain in my love, just as I have obeyed my
Father's commands and remain in his love" (John 15:10). In
other words, in keeping His Father's commandments, Jesus
stayed close to His Father and gave us a model for obeying
God's commands.

4. *Give your heart to Jesus*—Before anything...or anyone...
can grow, it must be alive. Therefore ask yourself a simple
question: Am I alive spiritually?

We read in Romans that

—*"all have sinned"* (3:23), that
—*"the wages of sin is death"* (6:23), and that
—*"God demonstrates his own love for us in this: While
we were still sinners, Christ died for us"* (5:8).

What this means is that you and I are sinners (there's no doubt about it!), which earned us the death penalty, but Jesus took on our sin and died in our place. As the words to one hymn ask, "Amazing love! How can it be, that Thou, my God, shouldst die for me?"[8] Think about it!

Getting It All Together

Here's another question for you as you move toward getting it all together—Have you accepted the wonderful truth of Christ's death on your behalf and named Jesus *your* Savior and the Lord of your life? Have you given Jesus your heart? As the Bible instructs, "If you confess with your mouth, 'Jesus is Lord,' and believe in your heart that God raised him from the dead, you will be saved" (Romans 10:9). Before you can experience any spiritual growth, this seed of faith in Jesus must take root in your heart and life.

So…are you alive?

Only three answers are possible—*no, I'm not sure,* and *yes*.

Answer #1: No—If you answered no—if you have not accepted Jesus as Lord and Savior—you can set foot on the path of walking with God and growing in Him right now by earnestly praying words like these from your heart. This is Step 1 toward getting your life together:

> Jesus, I know I am a sinner. I want to repent of my sins and turn and follow You. I believe You died for my sins and rose again victorious over the power of sin and death, and I want to

accept You as my personal Savior. Come into my life, Lord Jesus, and help me obey You from this day forward.

Answer #2: I'm not sure—If you aren't sure if the seed of faith has taken root in your heart, you may want to say a prayer of recommitment. You could pray words like these:

Jesus, I know that in the past I asked You into my life. I thought at that time that I was Your child, but my life hasn't shown the fruit of my belief. As I again hear Your call, I want to make a real commitment to You as the Lord and Master of my life.

Or perhaps the following prayer better fits your circumstances:

Dear Lord Jesus, I know that in the past I asked You into my life. I want to be Your child, I think and hope that I am Your child, but I want to *know* that I am Your child. Lord, give me the reassurance that I have eternal life through You because of Your death on the cross for my sin.

Whatever you do, if you're not sure where you stand with God, let Him know right now in a very personal prayer. Don't worry about the words. Just share your heart with Him. After all, God loves you, and He already knows your heart. He wants to be close to you.

Answer #3: Yes—Finally, if you answered—or can now

answer—"Yes! I know I'm alive in Christ now and forever!" take a few moments to thank God and praise Him for all that Jesus has done for you. Make a fresh commitment to walk with Jesus in obedience, to walk down the path of greater growth.

Heart Response

It's the prayer of my heart that God would use what's in this book to inspire you to grow in God's grace so that you are truly changed. Is that the desire of your heart too? Then I pray that you are moved to give yourself totally to Christ. May you seek nothing other than to follow Him, to walk with God.

Things to Do Today to Get It Going

In the chapters that follow you'll be given a list of "Things to Do Today" for getting started or improving on each fruit of the Spirit. In this chapter make your own list. Glance back through this chapter and write down three things you can do today to accelerate your walk with God. Be sure to write out exactly when you will do these things.

1.

2.

3.

Would You Like to Know More
About Walking by the Spirit?
Check It Out!

✓ What is God's call to you in Galatians 5:16?

What will be the result if and when you follow this instruction?

✓ According to Galatians 5:17, what conflict do believers live with?

Give one or two specific examples of your struggle in this area.

✓ Make a list of the "acts of the sinful nature" listed in Galatians 5:19-21.

Check the ones you struggle with most.

✓ Now list the fruit of the Spirit named in Galatians 5:22-23.

How do they differ from the "acts of the sinful nature"?

✓ Read John 15:1-8. Then review the section entitled "Discovering the Secret to Walking with God" and make a plan of action for how you will abide in Christ this week. Don't forget to be specific about when and how you will follow-through on your plan.

Getting the
Right Attitudes

2

A Loving Heart

The fruit of the Spirit is love.
Galatians 5:22

I don't think anyone—at least any female!—ever forgets a wedding. I can still clearly remember my daughter Courtney's marriage ceremony. After a whirlwind of busyness, family and friends joined me in watching a radiant and confident Courtney regally walk down the aisle in our church on her dad's arm. Soon Jim switched his dad hat to his minister's hat and summoned Courtney and her Paul to make a sober commitment to love each other for the rest of their days, to love one another with Christ's love.

Yes, I thought as I sat in the pew, *that's what God intends this wedding and all of life to be about—Christian love. He calls for a bride and groom to love one another. And He also calls each of His children to love parents and grandparents, brothers and sisters, uncles and aunts, and friends and enemies.*

Finding Out More About Love

We can't read very far in the New Testament without realizing that love is important to God. Grab your pen and note what you learn about love from these scriptures.

✎ *A Word from God's Word About Love...*

- "Live a life of love"—Ephesians 5:2

- "Love each other"—John 15:12

  God has called upon us
  to love one another.

- "Love our neighbor"—Matthew 22:39

  love other people with as much self love
  you have for yourself

- "Love our enemies"—Luke 6:27

  Show love to everyone, just
  not to the people we like.

As a child of God, you are to love others in the way you see it modeled by God and His Son. Exactly how has Jesus loved you? And what does the kind of love you're supposed to give to others look like? The Bible comes to your rescue and gives you principles that help you understand Christian love. Look now at five of these.

Principle #1: Love is an act of the will

Every fruit of the Spirit requires decisions, and love is no different. It's hard to love under stressful conditions, yet that's exactly where most of life is lived, isn't it? For instance, I don't know about you, but I especially need love when I'm tired, when I'm suffering in some way, when I'm hurting, or when I'm feeling burdened. At times like these, I usually don't feel up to loving other people. That's when—I'm learning—it's necessary to activate the will if I am to show love toward others. Christian love, you see, is an act of the will—a deliberate effort that we can make only by the grace of God. So we choose to...

- give love when we want to withhold,
- reach out to others when we are tired and want to rest,
- serve when we want to be served, and
- help others when we ourselves are hurting.

Thank the Lord for God's grace! This kind of love comes only from God, which He gives us to pass on to others. Think for a minute about these willful acts of love. In fact, get out your pen and jot down your thoughts about the instances that follow.

✎ *A Word from God's Word About Love...*

- *"God so loved the world that he gave his one and only Son"* (John 3:16);

- *"The Son of Man did not come to be served, but to serve, and to give his life"* (Matthew 20:28);

- Jesus *"resolutely set out for Jerusalem"* (Luke 9:51) where He would die for us.

Giving, serving, heading for Jerusalem, dying on a cross. These acts of love are acts of the will, not something done out of emotion. We have to remember that it is only as we look to God for His love that we can get the right attitude— a God attitude—and show hearts of love.

Principle #2: *Love is action—not just words*

Love is also something we do, not just the words we say. We are supposed to walk the walk, not just talk the talk. Yet acting in love is not always easy. As any woman—young or old—knows who gets tired and still has work or homework to do, who still needs to give a helping hand at home, watch over younger brothers and sisters, do some laundry, or go to a part-time job, love means that even when you and I are exhausted and can't wait to sit down and do nothing, we do our work, we serve, and we help others. You see, love has work to do, and love does that work. Love takes action—even when doing so requires strenuous effort. We are called to love, not with word or with tongue only, but "with actions and in truth" (1 John 3:18).

Do you realize every one of your family members gives you an opportunity to put on the work clothes of love and to serve? And love has work to do at school as well…or at your job…or at church…or anywhere there are people! So roll up your sleeves and challenge yourself to do the work of love. Show forth God's love not only by your words and attitudes but by your actions.

Principle #3: Love reaches out to the unlovely

Don't you find it's easy to love "the lovely"—nice, sweet people who say "thank you!" when you do something for them? Who appreciate you? Who are kind to you? But it's much harder to love "the unlovely." People who are mean and a pain are a real challenge when it comes to love.

Yet this is exactly what Jesus calls you to do. He said, "Love your enemies and pray for those who persecute you." When you do, you become like our "Father in heaven. He causes his sun to rise on the evil and the good, and sends rain on the righteous and the unrighteous" (Matthew 5:43-45).

Do you see it? God expects you to love the unlovely just as He does (like He does when He loves you and me!). God's love is never deserved—it simply is. And that's the kind of love you are to show to your enemies as well as to your friends, to the unlovely as well as to the lovely. Only the Holy Spirit at work in your life can help you to love like Jesus. Now that's the right attitude!

Principle #4: We need God to help us love

We need God's help for each of the fruit of the Spirit and love is no different. We rely on God for love. And do we ever need it for the tough ones—for the people who are unlovely! It's like this: Jesus said it's natural to love those who love us (Luke 6:32-33). But to love those who hate us is *super*natural. It's natural to hate our enemies, but as Christians we are called to the *super*natural—to love our enemies (Luke 6:35).

Think about this: Love "means that no matter what a man may do to us by way of insult or injury or humiliation we will never seek anything…but the best even for those who seek the worst for us."[1] Friend, only God can help us serve the very person who insults, snubs, or hurts us. And His love is right there, ready for you to give. (And remember, those who are hardest to love are the ones who usually need it most!)

Principle #5: Love expects nothing in return

Do you find that when you're nice to someone, you expect that person to be nice back to you? But Jesus tells us to do good to others "without expecting to get anything back" (Luke 6:35). To love as God loves is to love without any thought of payback or reward. It is to love as Jesus loved us—"A new command I give you: Love one another. As I have loved you, so you must love one another" (John 13:34).

Defining Love—Love Is "the Sacrifice of Self"

As these five principles of biblical love clearly reveal, love is *the sacrifice of self*. This simple definition crystalizes what the Bible teaches about love. As love has been explained, "Love is not an emotion. It is an act of self-sacrifice. It is not necessarily feeling loving toward a particular person. It may not have any emotion connected with it (Romans 5:8). God always defines biblical love in terms of self-sacrifice."[2] It's obvious then that since love is the sacrifice of self,

> Love involves effort, not merely emotion.
> Love demands action, not just feelings.
> Love is something we do, not something we only feel or say.

How are you doing when it comes to loving others by giving up something of yourself? As you look to God's Spirit to empower you to give His kind of love, pray along with St. Francis of Assisi, "O Divine Master, grant that I may not so much seek to be loved...as to love."

Living Out Love

When it comes to love, it helps me to see my call to live out love as an assignment from God to love anyone and everyone He puts in my path. It's sort of like the care I give to the flowers beside my front door. They are the first thing I see every morning when I open my door, and they are usually drooping and slumped over on the porch. One look tells me they need water in the worst way. So every day I get out my watering bucket, go to the faucet, fill up the bucket, and carry water to these poor little flowers. You see, if they don't get water, they'll die.

Through the years I've kept up what I call my "bucket brigade." I know that if I don't fill my bucket at the faucet and give my flowers life-giving water, they will die. I don't necessarily feel like watering them, but I do it anyway. I act on my will, not my feelings. I make the decision and put forth the effort to give the flowers water and keep them alive.

You and I can view the challenge of loving the people God puts in our path in the same way as I view caring for my flowers. We may not necessarily feel like loving them. But when we allow God to fill us up with His life-giving love, we can then carry His love to others and pour it out into their lives. The love is not ours—it's God's. But when we present our empty selves to Him—the Source of love— and are filled by Him, then we are able to share His love with thirsty, needy people. God is then able to pass on His love to others through us.

And I confess—I have my hard days! But on the hard days, when I frequently run dry, I go back to God over and over again so He can fill me again and again with His love for the people I encounter. For instance, when I offer a friendly greeting to a woman who doesn't respond, my flesh says, "Well, if that's what I get for being nice, forget it!" But I know that's exactly when I need to run to God and have Him fill me afresh with His love for that woman so I can share it with her. She is someone God wants to show His love to, and I can let Him do so through me. I can let myself be the vessel that carries His love to her! It's amazing isn't it?

Heart Response

Please be sure and spend some time praying to the God of love. Confess to Him all your unlovely thoughts about any unlovely people He has put in your life. Admit any wrong attitudes toward others. And ask for His help in getting the right attitude—an attitude of love...His love! Ask God to enable you to "love your enemies, do good to those who hate you, bless those who curse you, pray for those who mistreat you" (Luke 6:27-28). God wants to do that for you. You just need to open yourself up to receive from Him His endless supply of life-giving, life-changing love.

Things to Do Today to Walk in Love

1. Begin loving the people God puts in your path by first loving those people at home. As the saying goes, "What you are at home is what you are!" So be a woman who walks in God's love...at home.

2. Go to God throughout the day for a fresh supply of His love to share. At the first hint of decreasing love, look to the Lord of love.

3. Remember that your assignment from God is to serve (Galatians 5:13).

4. Remember Jesus, who "did not come to be served, but to serve, and to give his life as a ransom for many" (Matthew 20:28).

Would You Like to Know More
About Walking in Love?
Check It Out!

✓ Read 1 Corinthians 13:4-8a. Which part of love is most difficult for you to live out?

> Most of it. I need to work on 'love.'

Because fruit-bearing involves some effort on your part, what steps will you take this week toward overcoming that difficulty?

> Read 1 Corin. 13:4-8a, everyday, and read highlighter parts in this chapter. This way I will remember what love really is.

✓ According to 1 John 4:7-8, who is the source of love?

> God

What do verses 20 and 21 of that chapter say about how we can know if someone loves God?

> They love their brother

✓ What does Romans 5:5 teach about love?

God has poured out his love
to fufill us.

And Romans 5:8? God's love for us is
so great, even though we are sinners,
he loves us so much he was willing
to die.

✓ Who in your life is hardest to love and why?

The people I am jealous of, because
why should I want to show love,
joy to them when they have or
get what I want.

As you think about that person, read Jesus' words in Luke
6:27-28. What specific instructions about the person you
have in mind does Jesus give you here? I should
be a blessing & show love twords
her, even though its hard. Its what
Jesus would do.

What will you do this week to obey each of Jesus' commands? Don't forget to be specific!

I will read 1 Corinthians 13:4-8a
everyday to really get a good understanding
of what it really is, & try to demonstrate
God's love.

3

A Happy Heart

The fruit of the Spirit is...joy.
Galatians 5:22

One day my daughter Katherine received an unusual phone call from a business student at her college. He had started a little business of selling engagement rings to the guys on campus, and he was making a video catalog of diamonds and diamond rings. Steve had everything he needed to create his catalog—the diamonds, a studio, a camera, the lights. But he needed one more thing—a pair of hands. So he called to ask Katherine if she would come to the studio and model his rings.

So off Katherine went on the appointed taping day. When she arrived at the studio, Steve set up his camera and lights. Then he opened his jewel case and pulled out a piece of black velvet to serve as a backdrop for the diamonds. After turning on his studio lights, he removed the diamonds from his case, one by one for Katherine to model.

Next Steve instructed Katherine to slowly lift her hand up off the dark background toward the light as she modeled each ring. Steve explained, "When a diamond is placed against a dark background, the darkness makes it seem more brilliant. And when the diamond is lifted toward a light, all of its facets are revealed and allowed to sparkle." He said, "A diamond is pretty all by itself, but putting it against a black background and lifting it up to the light enhances its radiance and glory."

Oh, wow! What a perfect picture of joy! This is something we don't like to hear, but true spiritual joy shines brightest against the darkness of trials, tragedy, and testing. And the blacker the background, the greater the brilliance. In the same way, life's dark struggles make Christian joy more intense and our praise more glorious. As a poet reflected, God "sets in pain the jewel of His joy."

Finding Out More About Joy

Are you familiar with the book of Philippians in the Bible? It's a sparkling little epistle of joy. Just read it once and you'll notice its many references to joy, the next grace gift on God's list of the fruit of the Spirit. What do we learn about joy from the Bible, especially from the more than 70 New Testament references to it? It's pen or pencil time again. You'll be excited as you make notes while reading these truths and finding out more about joy!

✎ *A Word from God's Word About Joy...*

- *Joy is important to Jesus*—Shortly before His crucifixion, Jesus described the special relationship He would have with His disciples if they would abide in Him and His love. He ended His talk by saying, *"I have told you this so that my joy may be in you and that your joy may be complete"* (John 15:11). Jesus wanted His disciples to know the joy of fellowship with Him, joy to the fullest.

- *Joy is an expression of godliness*—You see, joy is a sure sign of the presence of God in our lives. Put differently, our joy is "the joy of God passing through a Christian,"[1] "a joy whose foundation is God."[2] As children of God, we have some great reasons to be joyful.

- *Joy is experienced anywhere and at any time*—How is this true? Because, as Philippians 4:4 tells us, we are to *"rejoice in the Lord always."* The phrase "in the Lord" points out the sphere in which our joy exists. "In the Lord" is a sphere that has nothing to do with our situation. No, instead it has everything to do with our relationship with Jesus. Because we take our relationship with Jesus everywhere we go, we can experience joy in

Him anywhere, anytime, no matter what's happening to us.

Discovering Three Good Reasons to Be Joyful

If this isn't enough to convince you about the importance of joy, look at these three reasons to be joyful. Keep your pen handy for making encouraging notes to yourself about how to have a happy heart, a more joyful life...or week...or day!

✎ *A Word from God's Word About Joy...*

- *Reason #1: Your joy is permanent*—Because your joy is rooted in your unchanging God, your joy is permanent. In John 16:22, Jesus says that *"no one will take away your joy."* However, one thing that can rob you of the joy God provides is your failure to walk with God. Therefore you are to *"live by the Spirit"* (Galatians 5:16). The Holy Spirit produces joy in your life as you abide in Christ and walk in obedience to His ways—as you walk by the Spirit.

- *Reason #2: Your joy is always available*—Since it's rooted in your faithful and ever-present God, your joy is always available. That's why you can *"rejoice in the Lord always"* (Philippians 4:4). Whatever the circumstances of your life, you have ready access to the source of true joy anytime you turn to God.

* *Reason #3: Your joy is also inexpressible*—That's how Peter described our joy in Jesus in 1 Peter 1:8: *"Though now you have not seen him, you love him; and even though you do not see him now, you believe in him and are filled with an inexpressible and glorious joy."* Joy in the Spirit is "joy beyond speech,"[3] "a foretaste of the joy of heaven,"[4] something which cannot be fully expressed or articulated.[5]

There is simply no way to explain why we experience joy when nothing in our life suggests we should be joyful!

Defining Joy—Joy Is "the Sacrifice of Praise"

It helps me to cultivate joy in my life by thinking of joy as *the sacrifice of praise.* Let me explain. When life is good, praise and thanksgiving flow freely from my heart and lips. But when life turns black, praise and thanksgiving don't flow quite so easily. Instead, I have to deliberately *choose* to follow God's advice and "give thanks in all circumstances, for this is God's will for you in Christ Jesus" (1 Thessalonians 5:18). Although I don't *feel* like praising the Lord or thanking

Him, I *do* what God says, and that effort makes my praise a sacrifice.

At times when I'd rather bask in self-pity or stay stuck in my depression, choosing to look beyond my pain makes my praise to God sacrificial. When I do lift such a sacrifice of praise to God out of the darkness of my trials, I find the Spirit's joy enlarged in my life—just as lifting a diamond to the light against a black background enhances its brilliance.

Caution! Joy Is Not an Emotion

Here's something else you must understand about true spiritual joy—It is not happiness. No, "happiness" is an emotion, a state of good fortune and success related to our circumstances. If all is going well, we are happy, but as soon as some dark cloud or irritation enters our life, our feeling of happiness vanishes.

I'm sure you're aware that pain is a fact of life. Contrary to our wishes, easy circumstances are not life's norm. Jesus warned, "In this world you will have trouble" (John 16:33). Paul explained, "Everyone who wants to live a godly life in Christ Jesus will be persecuted" (2 Timothy 3:12). In the midst of the reality of pain and sorrow, God's joy is a grace gift. He gives His joy to us as we encounter the hardships, tribulation, problems, and persecutions of life. Amazingly, this supernatural joy, given through God's Spirit, transcends all of the tough conditions of life.

As God's child through the new birth, you can experience and enjoy God's joy—regardless of what life offers you. You can be truly and genuinely happy…no matter what's going on around you. That's because your joy as a Christian…

- is not dependent on circumstances, but on the spiritual realities of God's goodness, His unconditional love for you, and His ultimate victory over sin and darkness.

- is not based on your efforts, accomplishments, or willpower, but rather on the truth about your relationship with the Father through the Son.

- is not merely an emotion, but the result of choosing to look beyond what appears to be true in your life to what is true about your life in Christ.

By now I'm sure you can see that your spiritual joy is not an experience that comes from favorable circumstances but is a sense of well-being that abides in the heart of the person who knows all is well between himself and the Lord.[6]

The Sources of Joy

Just as we take our empty self to God to be filled with His love, we also go to Him—the source of true joy—when we feel empty of Christian joy. Here are five reasons you can have that joy from Him. As you look through them, take your pen in hand and respond from your heart to the questions.

Reason #1: God Himself is a primary source of your joy— The psalmist reveals his heart's desire to "go to the altar of

God, to God my joy and my delight" (Psalm 43:4). Do you think of God as your "exceeding joy"? Do you turn to Him who lives in your heart for joy? God—the only source of true joy—wants to give you His joy. You need only to turn to Him to receive it. What can you do to turn to Him?

Reason #2: God's salvation—I'm sure you've noticed that when people share how they became Christians, they can't help but tell their story joyfully. Isaiah, for instance, could not contain his joy when he thought about all that God had done for him. He wrote, "I delight greatly in the LORD; my soul rejoices in my God. For he has clothed me with garments of salvation and has arrayed me in a robe of righteousness" (Isaiah 61:10). Now think of all that God has done for you. He paid a great price to obtain your salvation through His Son's death. There can be no greater joy than knowing you will live with God forever! Feel free to express your praise now.

Reason #3: God's promises—When my daughters were growing up, our family had a little plastic container shaped like a loaf of bread on our breakfast table. Each of the cards in that box had one promise from the Bible printed on it. Every morning one of us would close our eyes, reach over, pick a promise, and then read it as a part of our family devotions. Later that night at dinner, we would talk about that promise for the day again and how we had seen God be true to His Word since breakfast time.

Did you know that your Bible is like that plastic loaf of bread? It is filled with promises—as many (according to one calculation) as 8,000![7] Jot down one or more of your favorite promises. How often do you remember them, refer to them, use them to encourage your heart? And how does recalling them bring joy to your heart? If you are struggling with something right now, turn to the treasure of God's precious promises. Find joy in them.

Reason #4: Christ's kingdom—The fact that we who name Jesus as Savior and Lord have been welcomed into His kingdom brings great joy to the angels: "There is rejoicing in the presence of the angels of God over one sinner who repents" (Luke 15:10). Hearing others coming to Christ should evoke joy in you as well. Paul and Barnabas went from town to town describing the salvation of the Gentiles. The result? It caused great joy to all the brethren (Acts 15:3).

Do you need a dose of joy? Spend a few minutes recalling your own entrance into the kingdom of God. Share a few of the details of that wonderful day here. And if you have not yet tasted this heavenly joy, look again at pages 16 through 18. Perhaps today you will want to pray one of the prayers there from your heart.

Friend and sister, the joy of the Lord is available to you 24/7—24 hours a day, 7 days a week—any and every day, no matter what you're dealing with! Want joy? All you have to do is focus on God—not on your gloom, your tough life, the hard time someone gave you, your next exam. Just focus on God, on the eternal not the temporal. You experience the joy *of* the Lord when you go *to* the Lord and find your joy *in* the Lord. True joy—spiritual joy—is found only in the things of God. Ask God for His grace. Ask Him to help you remember to go to Him in your times of need to be filled with His joy.

Heart Response

Here's a fact of life: Until we are with the Lord, there will always be suffering. So...what trial is causing you the greatest grief, the sharpest pain, the deepest sorrow today? Is it a disappointment, a dashed dream, a disaster, a disability? Is it ridicule or persecution? A difficulty within your family? A strained relationship or an unknown future as you look down the road of life?

Whatever your greatest trial is today, let it cause you to turn to God for His joy. Let it cause you to offer Him a sacrifice of praise and allow you to be touched by Him, the only source of true joy. Your heart can be filled with genuine joy—spiritual joy—when you walk with God through your trials, praising Him with every step and breath. That's an attitude of joy!

Things to Do Today to Walk in Joy

1. Identify the trial that causes you the greatest grief. Name it here: *As of now, relashionships, (Mitch)*

2. Copy Hebrews 13:15 from your Bible. Then offer to God the sacrifice of your praise concerning your heartbreaking situation...even if it is offered with tears.

   "Through Jesus, therefore, let us continually offer to God a sacrifice of praise - the fruit of lips that confess his name." (Heb. 13:15)

3. Read James 1:2-4 and Romans 5:1-5. Then follow James' advice and consider that trial a joy. Write down what you think God is teaching you through this trial. What good has already come into your life as a result of it?

   I think God is trying to show me two things. 1st, I cannot be in a real relashionship until my relashionship with God is strong. I need to improve on that relashionship before any other. 2nd, I think God is telling me find a Christian boy, not one who isint. Someone who puts the lord first.

Would You Like to Know More About Joy? Check It Out!

✓ Read 1 Samuel 1:9-18. List some of Hannah's problems.

She wants a son

What made the difference in Hannah's attitude, and how was it changed? Hannah's attitude changes from sadness to joy because she praied to the Lord, and found strength in him.

✓ Read 1 Samuel 1:19–2:1. How did Hannah fulfill her vow? When God gave her a son, she sacrificed him.

Write out Hannah's sacrifice of praise in 2:1.

"My heart rejoices in the Lord; in the Lord my horn is lifted high. My mouth boasts over my enimes for I delight in your deliverances"

What was her source of joy?

The Lord

What circumstances in Hannah's life could have caused her to be sorrowful?

She didn't have a son.

What do you learn about joy from Hannah?

That her joy came from the Lord.

✓ Read Acts 16:22-25. List some of Paul's problems.

he was stripped, beaten, & put in Jail

What did Paul do to experience and show His joy in the Lord? *Sing hymns'.*

✓ List some of your problems.

- Not being able to make friends on dance team
- Caring to much about peoples opinions

As you think about Hannah and Paul, what can you do right this minute...and this week...to experience the joy of the Lord? *Pray & worship him.*

4

A Quiet Heart

The fruit of the Spirit is...peace.
Galatians 5:22

A famous newspaper columnist and counselor, Ann Landers, was once asked if any
one problem stood out in the more than
10,000 letters she received in the mail each
week. Her answer? Fear.

Doctors also know the results of fear in their patients. The
first symptom of illness is not always a cough or chest pain,
but fear, which sooner or later shows up as a clinical
symptom.

Causes for fear surround us on every side. But here's
good news for us as Christians: We have a built-in resource
for handling fears. That resource is the peace of God. And
what a refreshing fruit God's peace is in a mad, mad, mad,
mad world! Life is like a roller coaster, but we can experience God's peace—no matter what is happening in our

lives—when we walk by His Spirit. We are blessed with "the peace of God, which transcends all understanding" (Philippians 4:7) right in the very middle of our trials when we look to God for it.

Finding Out More About Peace

Many people think of peace as the absence of problems. They equate peace with the feeling they experience when all is well, when there are no issues or problems or pains. But the peace of the Lord is not related to circumstances at all. In fact, God's peace comes to us and endures...regardless of life's circumstances.

Peace is like this. Our daughter Courtney and her husband, Paul, lived on Kauai, Hawaii, the island that experienced the fierce Hurricane Iniki. When Jim and I drove around the island on a visit there, we saw the evidence of destruction. In fact, you can still see it there today. But we also saw the huge warning sirens on every beach and in every town. We could well imagine the fear the islanders must have felt as those sirens wailed on the day the killer Hurricane Iniki approached. But we could also imagine the peace they must have felt when those same devices finally sounded the all-clear signal.

Now, can you imagine having the same perfect peace whether the sirens are signaling a storm or the hurricane is actually roaring around you? That's the kind of peace God offers to you for the many storms of life. Notice these truths about this peace that comes from God. Better yet, take pen in hand and note your thoughts and observations. Circle and underline what you like or find interesting.

- Our peace has nothing to do with our circumstances, and everything to do with knowing we have a right relationship with God.[1]

- Our peace has nothing to do with daily challenges or crises, and everything to do with knowing that our times are in God's hands.[2]

- Our peace has nothing to do with the conditions of our lives, and everything to do with knowing that God is all-sufficient.[3]

- Our peace is an inward repose and serenity of soul that indicates a heart at rest—regardless of our circumstances—as we place complete confidence in God minute by minute.

Now, keep your pen or pencil in hand as you make your way through these facts and scriptures.

✎ *A Word from God's Word About Peace...*

- Peace comes with knowing that your heavenly Father is continually with you—and indeed He is! God is omnipresent, everywhere at once, and fully aware of every detail of your life—at every moment and in every place. He knows your needs at all times and in every situation. In Psalm 139:7-10, David declared that *"if I go up to the heavens, you are there; if I make my bed in the depths, you are there...if I...settle on the far side of the sea, even there your hand will guide me."* Dear younger sister, you can never be any place—from the heights of heaven to the depths of the sea and everywhere in between— where God is not present with you and available to you. Therefore, the key to your peace is not the absence of conflict. No, it's the presence of God, no matter what the conflict.[4] Wow, just let that truth wash over you for a minute!

- Peace also comes with acknowledging that God will supply your every need. For instance, when Paul asked Jesus to remove the thorn in his flesh and Jesus said no, Paul learned the truth of Jesus' statement: *"My grace is sufficient for you"* (2 Corinthians 12:9). Paul learned the truth he wrote in Philippians 4:19—*"God will meet all your needs according to his glorious riches in Christ Jesus"*—and, in 2 Corinthians 9:8, that *"God is able to make all grace abound to you, so that in all things at all times, having all that you need, you will abound in every good work."* Do you realize what these promises mean? They mean that you will never have a real need that God is not able to meet. This, my friend, is another *wow!*

Defining Peace—Peace Is "the Sacrifice of Trust"

I like to think of peace as *the sacrifice of trust*. You see, you and I make the sacrifice of trust when we face pain and stress in our lives and choose to trust God instead of panicking or falling apart. When circumstances in your life might tempt you to panic, feel terrified, become a nervous wreck, or be filled with dread, you can choose to either give in to those feelings or trust in God, presenting yourself to Him to be filled with His peace. You can either trust Almighty God or succumb to the emotions of the flesh. Choosing to trust God—making the sacrifice of trust—causes you to experience His peace...even in the midst of tremendous uproar.

Here's how it works. We make the sacrifice of trust and experience God's peace...

when we choose not to panic... but to rest in God's presence,

> when we release our terror… and trust in God's
> wisdom and ways, when we reject our nerv-
> ousness…and remember that God is in con-
> trol, and when we ignore our dread…and
> instead accept God's dealings.

Now imagine…taking your next exam full of peace instead of panic. Imagine…trying out for a part in a play or the pep squad or auditioning for the orchestra or choir and completely trusting God for the outcome. Imagine…giving your speech or making an announcement in front of your classmates without a worry in the world. Sister, that's peace! God's kind of peace.

Getting God's Peace

Are you wondering how to get this peaceful attitude, the attitude of a heart at rest? Well, you get it in the same way you get all the other fruit. When you are filled with the Holy Spirit and walking in God's ways, you will have the peace that comes from God—and from God alone. You will have a quiet heart.

Don't you just love receiving gifts? Well, pick up your pen again and unwrap these four gifts from God. They contain four sources for God's peace. Be sure and make your own set of notes as you read.

Gift #1: God, the Son—Before Jesus was even born, the Old Testament prophet Isaiah predicted, "For to us a child is born, to us a son is given…and he will be called…Prince of Peace" (Isaiah 9:6). That name reflects Jesus' mission.

- His death on Calvary gave believers the gift of peace with God that comes only with forgiveness for sins.

- His work on the cross paved the way for personal peace with God.

- His coming to earth accomplished salvation for those who put their trust in Christ.

As Romans 5:1 states, "Since we have been justified through faith, we have peace with God through our Lord Jesus Christ."

Gift #2: God the Father—Through the Bible, you can get to know God. You can learn all about His promises and His faithfulness so that you may trust Him in your times of need. One of those promises is found in Isaiah 26:3: "You will keep in perfect peace him whose mind is steadfast, because he trusts in you." As you know, there's no way you can avoid strife as you walk in the world, but you can know perfect peace in the midst of turmoil as you turn to God Himself instead of focusing on your difficulties.

Gift #3: God's Word—The Bible helps you know God by revealing His law, His ways, and His purposes. When you follow God's Word and walk in His ways, you experience His peace to the point that nothing causes you to stumble. "Great peace have they who love your law, and nothing can make them stumble" (Psalm 119:165). You experience the peace that comes with keeping a right relationship with God.

Gift #4: God, the Spirit—The Holy Spirit is your personal Helper, Teacher, and Comforter (John 14:26). Jesus said, "The Counselor, the Holy Spirit, whom the Father will send in my name, will teach you all things and will remind you of everything I have said to you." And what is the blessed result of this gift? "Peace I leave with you; my peace I give you. I do not give as the world gives. Do not let your heart be troubled and do not be afraid" (verse 27). The instruction, guidance, and comfort you receive from God's Spirit promotes your peace. When you abide in Christ and walk by His Spirit, this peace from God is yours.

Doesn't this make you want to pause and give thanks to God for these four gifts? Just think about it. As a Christian, you can look to God—the Father, the Son, and the Holy Spirit—and to God's Word for peace. Bless His name and thank Him profusely!

Walking on the Path of Peace

Now that you know more about God's peace, what can you do to live in such a way that you can cultivate this gift of His Spirit?

- You can *pray*. Pray first, pray often, and pray continually. When you pray and place your worries, fears, doubts, and concerns into God's hands, you'll be spending time in the presence of the Lord. You'll enjoy fellowshiping with Him, worshiping Him, learning from Him, and leaning on Him—and, yes, experiencing His peace.

- You can *pause* and turn to the Lord when a crisis or disaster comes along. When you pause to acknowledge God—His presence, His all-sufficiency, His power, His love—He will make your paths straight. And blessing upon blessing, once you've turned to Him, you will again be in touch with His tremendous peace.

- You can *peruse* the gospels (Matthew, Mark, Luke, John). Read and study Jesus' life to see the peace He experienced in stressful situations. You can learn how abiding in the Father directed Jesus' thoughts, words, deeds, responses, and reactions in difficult circumstances. You can carry Jesus' attitudes in your mind as you go to school, do your work and homework, interact with people of all kinds, and seek to live in peace with those at home. Jesus' example will help you walk in peace.

Heart Response

Are you longing for this kind of heart—a quiet heart, a heart at rest, a heart of peace? Then take an "attitude" exam. What has an outside observer seen in you this week? Are you in turmoil...or are you trusting in God and at peace? Are you running around in circles...or are you resting in the Lord? Are your words revealing a sense of panic and pressure...or are they words that help and encourage others? Are your actions reflecting the priorities God has set for you? Is your relationship with Him first...or are you too busy to sit at His feet and enjoy His presence?

Remember, your assignment from God is to get the right attitudes going in your life! And every day is a test. Are you improving?

Things to Do Today to Walk in Peace

1. Do yourself (and everybody else!) a favor and identify the issue that repeatedly causes you to stress out. For instance, what worry keeps you awake at night? What concern sets your mind churning and your heart fretting as the alarm clock jars you awake each morning? What problem weighs you down or never goes away?

2.   Make the conscious decision to trust this problem to God. Pray and make the sacrifice of trust. This will allow your heart to rest in Him and enable you to experience His peace—even in this, your most difficult challenge.

Would You Like to Know More About Peace? Check It Out!

✓ Read Psalm 139. List what you learn about God.

List what you learn about God's knowledge of you, your whereabouts, and your situation.

List three things you want to remember about God the next time you are in a trying or lonely situation and in need of God's peace.

1.

2.

3.

✓ Read Luke 8:22-25 and Mark 4:35-41. Describe the scene in these passages. What was going on? Who was there?

How did the disciples react to the situation?

What was Jesus doing, and how did He respond to the situation? To the disciples?

How was Jesus' peace evidenced?

List three lessons you want to remember about trusting God in difficult times.

1.

2.

3.

5

Looking at Jesus' Attitudes

Think now for a few minutes about the three chapters on love, joy, and peace. They were about the circumstances of life that call for us, as God's women, to display these spiritual fruits. To review,

- a need for *love* is created by ill treatment, hostility, abuse, and hatred.

- a need for *joy* springs from sorrow, tribulation, tragedy, affliction, and trials.

- a need for *peace* comes as we face the events in life that evoke panic, fear, terror, dread, and anxiety.

Unfortunately these circumstances seem to come all too often. But oh, how blessed we are to be able to follow the example of Jesus, who faced these same fruit-bearing opportunities! Take a close look now at Jesus in the Garden of Gethsemane, where we see Him living out all three godly attitudes...love, joy, and peace...despite the events He faced. I found these words that help us understand all that happened that night before Jesus' journey to the cross:

> Ever and always the teacher, Jesus used even this struggle with the enemy in the garden the night before the cross to teach the disciples and every future believer another lesson in godliness, a lesson about facing temptation and severe trial. The Lord not only was preparing Himself for the cross but also, by His example, preparing His followers for the crosses He calls them to bear in His name.[1]

Now, allow Jesus to teach you as we peer into this dark night, which was also the most spiritually dark night in human history. That was the night the sinless Son of God faced death for your sins and mine in order to accomplish our salvation. Be aware as you read about this sacred scene from the Savior's life that you are truly standing on holy ground! Jesus' life on earth is nearing its end, and He faces every ugly word and evil deed ever directed at a person. Through God's provision of the four gospels, we are allowed to witness exactly how Jesus handled this hatred, sorrow, and trauma.

The Plan

Throughout His three years of teaching, Jesus often referred to God's plan for His death, which always caused bewilderment in His disciples. For instance, in John 7:6 Jesus said, "The right time for me [to die] has not yet come." But as Jesus prepared for His final Passover meal, He clearly stated the opposite: "My time is at hand" (Matthew 26:18 KJV). It was time for Him to die and to fulfill the Father's plan. All was in place. Judas, the traitor, had already been dismissed to do the evil deed of betraying his Master. As it neared midnight, Jesus prayed His high priestly prayer for and with His disciples (John 17). After they sang a hymn (Matthew 26:30), Jesus "left with his disciples and crossed the Kidron Valley. On the other side there was an olive grove, and he and his disciples went into it" (John 18:1).

The Purpose

What drove Jesus to the Garden of Gethsemane? It was His situation. It was this crossroad in His life. It was the challenge He faced during His final days. His time had finally come—and what was ahead? Betrayal by His disciples. Misunderstanding from His family and followers. Rejection from mankind. Hostility and persecution. An angry mob, angry leaders, and angry people. Verbal and physical assault. An unjust sentence. The excruciating pain of crucifixion. Death. And worst of all, momentary separation from His heavenly Father. From a human perspective, Jesus was losing all He had—His life, His family, His ministry, His friends, and His personal dignity.

Yet His heavenly Father had commanded that He die for these sinners—and Jesus obeyed. Doing so would benefit others—including you and me—because His death would be for sinners like us. So acting in love, Jesus gave Himself as a sacrifice, as a ransom for others (Matthew 20:28).

The Place

Facing the overwhelming challenge of the cross, Jesus went to Gethsemane (Matthew 26:36). This place was probably a secluded spot, walled in and containing some olive trees. Jesus had gone there often with His disciples (John 18:2) because it was quiet, a good spot for teaching, prayer, rest, and sleep. On the eve of His death, Jesus retreated to this familiar place of prayer with His little band of followers.

The People

After He entered the place called Gethsemane, Jesus did two things. First, He asked eight of the disciples to "sit here while I go over there and pray" (Matthew 26:36). Jesus left these men outside the wall or gate of the garden as lookouts. Next Jesus invited three of the disciples—Peter, James, and John—to go along with Him to pray.

The Problems

Disappearing into the black darkness, Jesus began the battle. The Father's plan caused Him deep distress, and the Bible gives us glimpses into His extensive *emotional* anguish. Jesus cried out, "My soul is overwhelmed with sorrow, to the point of death" (Matthew 26:38). He "began to be deeply distressed and troubled" (Mark 14:33), so much so that He fell upon the ground in prayer. Luke tells us that He was "in anguish" (22:44). Our Lord "offered up prayers and petitions with loud cries and tears" (Hebrews 5:7). As one scholar writes, "All the waves and the billows of distress came pouring over His soul."[2]

God's command to die also caused Jesus to suffer terrible physical stress: "Being in anguish, he prayed more earnestly, and his sweat was like drops of blood falling to the ground" (Luke 22:44).

Jesus was fighting another great battle in addition to these emotional and physical struggles, and that was the spiritual war. Knowing this, Jesus had instructed His companions to "watch and pray so that you will not fall into temptation" (Matthew 26:41). Our Lord threw Himself upon the mercy of His Father and uttered, "My Father, if it is possible, may this cup [of death] be taken from me" (verse 39). On the physical level, Jesus wanted the cup taken away. No one has ever desired to taste death, and neither did Jesus. But from the spiritual perspective, He wanted to do His Father's will and therefore added to His plea, "Yet not as I will, but as you will" (verse 39).

The Process

With this submission to God's will, we see Jesus emerge triumphant from His agonizing struggle in the Garden. How did He gain the victory? How did Jesus remain steadfast in the love, joy, and peace that compelled Him to willingly die for sinners? What kept Him from giving in to physical and emotional desires? What was the process? And what can we learn so that we, too, can grow in love, joy, and peace?

Love is the sacrifice of self. For love, Jesus looked to God, the Father, who had commanded Him to die for sinners. And in love, Jesus reached out to the Father for His sustaining and strengthening love. He offered *the sacrifice of self* and determined to do the Father's will. Jesus' love looked to the Father—and looked at us—and the Spirit enabled Him to submit to death on a cross (Hebrews 9:14). The *flesh* wanted to avoid the trial and pain ahead, but *love* turned to the Father and said, "Not as I will, but as you will" (Matthew 26:39). That decision led to severe and intense suffering… and our salvation.

Joy offers the sacrifice of praise. In joy, Jesus lifted praise to God. The Bible tells us that Jesus experienced great joy: "for the joy set before him [in the Father and by the Father, He] endured the cross, scorning its shame" (Hebrews 12:2).

Peace comes with the sacrifice of trust. For peace, Jesus left His problems with God. "The peace of God, which transcends all understanding" (Philippians 4:7) rushed to guard Jesus' heart and mind, and He got up off that holy, tear-stained, sweat-drenched ground to go on in peace, knowing His times were in the Father's hands, saying in all peace and with total trust, "Let us go!" (Matthew 26:46).

The Product

And now please note, nothing about Jesus' circumstances

changed! After agonizing in prayer, he was still going to go to the cross, still going to be crucified, still going to die. But He went to the cross sustained by God's love, joy, and peace.

And note something else: This transformation, this acceptance, this turning point, was not accomplished with a snap of Jesus' fingers, the wink of His eye, or the wave of any wand. It came because Jesus went to the Father—in agony and with blood and sweat and tears. Lying face down on the earth in literal darkness as He fought the deeper darkness that settled upon His soul, Jesus looked to His Father for the Father's love, the Father's joy, and the Father's peace.

Jesus' ultimate submission to God's will did not come easily. One time in prayer was not enough (Matthew 26:39). Two times was not enough (verse 42). No, Jesus turned to the Father three separate times (verse 44). And these three times in prayer were not the flinging of trite thoughts toward heaven! They were more like three hour-long sessions (Matthew 26:40) of agonizing, wrestling, struggling, and fighting so that He could do all that God required of Him.

When our Savior finally rose to go forward and face the cross, He did so with love, with joy, and with peace. Filled with these graces, the Son declared, "Let us go!" (Mark 14:42).

The Performance

Oh, dear younger sister in Christ! We've just seen Jesus submit to His Father's will—to death on the cross! We cannot help but stop to marvel! This is too amazing for us not to pause…and to praise…and to pray! Oh, dear Jesus, thank You!

But we must also look to ourselves and to our walk with God. How is your performance when it comes to following God's direction for your life? Speaking for myself, I know I pray so little. When something tough comes along in my day, I too often blurt out, "No way!" and go on my merry way. If something requires more than I want to give, I say, "Oh, thank you very much, but I won't be able to do that." Or I grind on, doing what I have to do—on my own, in my own flesh, and by my own power—never approaching the Father for His filling. I murmur, gripe, complain, and fret. I do my duty…but I do it grudgingly. And I do it without love, joy, and peace.

In times like these, I need to follow my Lord's example and go to my Garden of Gethsemane. I need to pray. I need to turn to the Father and fight with my flesh until I realize His fruit of love, joy, and peace. I need to spend the time—however long it takes—to allow Him to fill me with Himself until I have all of Him and He has all of me.

If you and I would, for one week or even one day, commit ourselves to God in this way—if we would rush to Him in prayer and remember His promises when we need love, when we need joy, and when we need peace, and stay there until we have it, however long it takes—we could indeed change our world for Christ. If we would commit ourselves to spend time in the Garden with the Father and to pay the price to walk by the Spirit, overcome the flesh, and thereby experience God's love and joy and peace...

Well, the effects are unknown, untold, and limitless! Prayer in our own garden would mean Christ in us changing our hearts, our relationships, our families, our friends, our neighborhoods, our schools, and our world. And He can do it! But without Him, we can do nothing (John 15:5). Without Him, we only go through the motions, giving so little to our family, a friend, a stranger, or a world that needs so much.

Here's my personal prayer for growth in these three attitudes of love, joy, and peace. I pray it will become yours as well as you visit the garden often as you walk along life's way, where you seek the right attitudes—Jesus' attitudes.

> It is in prayer, Father,
> That we press ourselves to You,
>   O All-Sufficient One,
> That we get...in order to give,
>   that we petition...in order to praise,
>   that we wrestle...in order to rest.
> We must have our time in the garden.
> We must go to Gethsemane...
>   daily...first...often, if need be.
>
> May we hold high in our hearts and minds
>   this picture of Jesus in the Garden.

Impress it upon our souls.
May we follow in His steps
    and refuse to rise until we have
      Your love...Your joy...Your peace.
We pray in Jesus' name, who has taught us
    how to pray. Amen.

Would You Like to Know More About Jesus? Check It Out!

✓ Read Matthew 20:28. According to these words spoken by Jesus, what was the purpose of His life on earth?

Write out Matthew 20:28 on a card to carry with you and to memorize. Allow its truth to permeate your heart as you walk in the steps of Jesus.

✓ What do you learn about Jesus' prayer life from...
Matthew 6:6?

Matthew 26:36 and John 18:2?

Mark 1:35?

✓ How earnest are Jesus' prayers in these verses?
Matthew 26:37-38—

Mark 14:33—

Luke 22:44—

Hebrews 5:7—

What command did Jesus give His disciples in Matthew 26:41?

How can you obey this command?

✓ Write out Jesus' prayer in Matthew 26:39. What was the attitude of His heart?

Getting Along
with Everybody

6

A Time to Do Nothing

The fruit of the Spirit is...patience.
Galatians 5:22

Each day as I seek to walk with God, I (probably like you) try to design a schedule that will guarantee a devotional time with God each morning. On a really good day, when the alarm clock goes off in the morning I hop out of bed full of good intentions and solid plans and I experience Victory #1—I got up!

It feels so good to be up and in control of my day (so far, anyway!). What a blessing to enter into God's presence, to read His Word, and to linger in prayer. And then I experience Victory #2—I had my quiet time!

Next I start in on my daily chores. Usually my happy spiritual condition extends to serving others under my roof in a variety of ways—getting someone a glass of juice, helping with breakfast and clean up, making lunches while humming, and doing whatever it takes to get others out the door and off to school or work. As everyone waves goodbye for the day, I experience Victory #3—I got to help others make a good start on their day. I think to myself, *This is great! All is well! I'm on a roll. What a wonderful day this is going to be!*

But then real life—the rest of the day—begins. You know, a day of dealing with people—and all the joys and sorrows that can bring. It usually gets pretty intense! Also, in real life the phone rings (a lot!), and I have to take care of the person and the details of each call. Most calls go well, but there are those problem calls. Someone's upset with me. Or the person on the phone says something that hurts me. Sometimes the caller reports something someone else has said. I may even learn that I've been rejected in some way.

Pain comes in a variety of packages—through a letter in the mail...or a visitor to the house...or by telephone. And when the package is opened, you and I are left confused, wounded, bewildered, baffled, and hurting. We may feel used or abused, dumped on or manipulated, heart-sick or sorrowful. There was an insult, an accusation, a disagreement, an argument, a criticism, maybe even a physical blow. Now what are we supposed to do? Now what can we do to keep on walking with God? To experience more victories?

Thank God that He gives us three more graces, three more pieces of fruit—patience, kindness, and goodness (Galatians 5:22)—for managing the strain of personal relationships, for getting along with everyone—even with difficult people.

Listening to God's Call to Patience

It's good to realize up front that as Christians you and I are called by God to be patient. Get your pen out again. You may want to make notes about God's instructions.

✎ *A Word from God's Word About Patience...*

- The Bible instructs us to *"clothe [ourselves] with...patience"* (Colossians 3:12). That means we are to adorn ourselves with hearts of patience. Just as we dress our bodies every day by putting on clothes, we are to dress our spirits each morning with the godly quality of patience. Imagine how lovely and beautiful it is to be robed with God's patience! Can you think of someone who seems to be robed with patience? What do you see in his or her life?

- The Bible says Christians are to *"be patient"* (Ephesians 4:1-2). We better our relationships with other believers and promote unity when we conduct our lives with patience. How do we do this? By being patient when we see faults in other people or are annoyed by them in any way...instead of being irritated or critical or lashing out. Who is it that irritates you most and why? What can—and will—you do to be more patient with them?

• The Bible tells us the source of patience: We are to be *"strengthened with all power according to his glorious might so that you may have great endurance and patience"* (Colossians 1:11). According to this verse, what can—and will—you do to develop greater patience?

Patience isn't easy. But it is definitely a key to harmony in relationships. Patience is a practical first step to getting along with people. But before we can turn that key it will help us to understand the meaning of godly patience.

Finding Out More About Patience

If you're like me, you probably think of patience as being able to wait and wait and wait a very loooong time! But much more is involved in the kind of patience that is a fruit of the Spirit. Suppose patience were available in a can at the grocery store. What divine ingredients would be written on the label?

Ingredient #1—The first and primary ingredient in patience is *endurance.* The old King James word "longsuffering" paints the picture of patience pretty clearly for us. This ingredient of patient endurance is practiced primarily toward people and relates to our attitude toward others.[1] "It is the quality of putting up with other people, even when...sorely tried!"[2]

Ingredient #2—Next comes a very special condition that requires patience: *when injured.* You see, we need patience to endure injuries inflicted by others,[3] a patience that is characterized by longsuffering, evenness of temper, or patient endurance when injured by another.[4] As one source explains, "Patience is that calm and unruffled temper with which the good [person] bears the evils of life…[that] proceed from [others]."[5] So when your tolerance level wears thin, remember "real love…is patient, and it never gives up."[6]

Ingredient #3—Another ingredient in patience is *mercy*. God's patience is always connected with mercy[7] and bears with others for their good.[8] Patience wishes well to others and is willing to endure with them…hoping for their good.

Think about patience as you read these words: "If God had been a man, He would have wiped out this world long ago, but He has that patience which bears with all of our sinning and will not cast us off. [Therefore] in our dealings with our fellow men we must reproduce this loving, forbearing, forgiving, patient attitude of God."[9] Wow! We are actually acting like God when we are patient with people!

And why does God delay the punishment of man? The Bible explains that "the Lord is not slow in keeping his promise [to come again], as some understand slowness. He is patient with you, not wanting anyone to perish, but everyone to come to repentance" (2 Peter 3:9). In other words, the Lord is waiting to come again. He is desiring for more souls to believe and come to salvation. He's giving mankind an extended opportunity to receive Christ! Like God, we should be consumed with the same thought for others: "If I just wait long enough, maybe something good and wonderful will happen to this person!"

Ingredient #4—Finally, written in red letters across the label on our can of patience are these words: "Contains no anger or vengeance!" There is no wrath or thought of revenge or retaliation in God's kind of patience. Patience is the grace of the man who *could* revenge himself but *chooses* not to.[10] God tells us, "Do not take revenge...but leave room for God's wrath, for it is written: 'It is mine to avenge; I will repay,' says the Lord" (Romans 12:19).[11]

Patience withholds. It withholds vengeance, revenge, and retaliation...and endures instead.

Defining Patience—Patience "Does Nothing"

With these ingredients in mind, the definition of patience I use for myself is "Patience does nothing." Patience is the front end of these three fruit that relate to people—patience, goodness, and kindness—and it is the passive part of love.[12] It is love doing nothing.

Please, don't worry or wonder! Just hold on! In the next two chapters we'll move up the "action scale" of fruit-bearing when it comes to getting along with everyone. But for now,

> if you want to walk in patience
> when you've been hurt,
> wronged, or
> ill-treated,
> do nothing!

Don't react! Don't do something negative and harmful and sinful. Instead, resist in patience. *Doing nothing* gives you time (even a second!) to *do something*—to pray, to reflect, to ask for advice, and to plan to respond in a good, better, or best way. First go to God for His patience...and then do nothing that will cause you to lose His precious patience. (And just a hint—this process is usually accomplished by praying!)

Waiting for the Judge

One evening while I was teaching on this fruit of the Spirit, I talked to my class about how to grow in God's patience. I told my students to remember to wait for the judge. Let me explain. (And this is a good time to pick up your pen! You'll want to note this concept well!)

✎ *A Word from God's Word About Patience...*

- In an encouraging passage written to a group of poor and persecuted Christians, the apostle James appealed to these saints to...

  "be patient...until the Lord's coming" (James 5:7),

  "be patient...because the Lord's coming is near" (verse 8),

  "the Judge is standing at the door!" (verse 9).

Here's the message: When the Lord does arrive, things will most definitely change (Revelation 21:3-4)! Your suffering at the hands of others will be over. You will enjoy the continuing presence of Jesus. And He, the Judge, will also take vengeance upon your enemies. Indeed, everything will be made right as Christ brings justice and avenges the righteous. How does this encourage you in your suffering today?

- However, until our Lord, the Judge, arrives to settle things, you are to live with your adversaries and endure ill treatment from difficult people...while remaining patient and practicing self-restraint. You are not to turn to self-pity or complaining (see James 5:7-9). And you are not to judge, quarrel, criticize, gossip, or find fault. No, you are responsible for only one thing while you wait, and that is Christlike conduct. The Judge is responsible for everything else! How do you tend to react to mistreatment by others, and what better way will you put into practice?

- With this image in mind, ask yourself, "Can I wait?" James says you can! So pick the person in your life who has caused you the most personal pain. You know, the person who is hostile, mean, or ungrateful, who ignores you, insults you, slanders you, or blocks your progress. Then—through prayer and by God's grace and His help—resist every urge to retaliate or punish that person and instead do nothing. In patience, do nothing while you wait for the Judge.

Heart Response

Think about your struggles with patience for a minute. Which is easier—to give in to emotions and anger when someone has hurt you or to practice patience and hold back your wrath? To lash out with cruel words or to hold back your hateful words? Amazingly, it's no problem to let go, lose your temper, and tell your offender exactly how you feel and what you think! But much harder is the godly response—God's response!—of choosing to do nothing outwardly as you resist in patience inwardly. Believe me, it takes all of God's strength and grace to help you do nothing! You desperately need God's Spirit to fill you with His patience. (And so do I!) But once you're filled, then doing nothing as you resist in patience is how you practice patient endurance... when you're injured by others...without vengeance...and for their good! That's God's recipes for patience.

Things to Do Today to Walk in Patience

1.   Train yourself in longsuffering. Proverbs 19:11 says, "A man's wisdom gives him patience; it is to his glory to

overlook an offense." In other words, learn to restrain your anger.

2. Lengthen your fuse. How long can you wait? Make that period a little longer. How many times can you wait? Make it a few more times next time. That's where prayer comes into play. Our patient God is willing to give you His patience whenever you ask for it.

3. Remove opportunities to sin. As Paul counsels, "Do not think about how to gratify the desires of the sinful nature" (Romans 13:14). And Proverbs says that "it is to a man's honor to avoid strife, but every fool is quick to quarrel" (20:3). Carefulness can keep you from sinning.

4. Follow Jesus' example. He remained absolutely sinless even under the most severe mistreatment. "He committed no sin, and no deceit was found in his mouth. When they hurled their insults at him, he did not retaliate; when he suffered, he made no threats" (1 Peter 2:22-23). Carry Jesus' response to suffering in your

heart and mind...and try to lift your own responses to a higher level of Christ-likeness.

5.   Pray. This was Jesus' surefire method for enduring His suffering. He "entrusted himself to him who judges justly" (1 Peter 2:23). When you are injured by others, turn your aching soul heavenward. With God's help, be patient with others for their own good.

*Would You Like to Know More
About Patience?
Check It Out!*

✓ Read Genesis 6:3-5. What did God observe about mankind (verse 5)?

How long did He wait for the inhabitants of the earth to change their ways (verse 3)?

✓ Read 1 Peter 3:20, and write out the words that describe the patience of God.

✓ Read 1 Peter 2:22-23. Describe Jesus' perfect, sinless conduct (verse 22).

Yet how was He treated (verse 23)?

How did Jesus exhibit patience toward those who put Him to death?

✓ Read 2 Timothy 2:24-26. Write out the different words and phrases that indicate patience (verse 25).

What might be the outcome of such patience according to verses 25-26?

✓ Read 1 Thessalonians 5:14. What bottom-line principle for patience is stated here?

✓ As you review the teaching from these scriptures regarding patience, list three things you want to remember—or remember to do—to better handle your people problems.

A Time to Do Something

The fruit of the Spirit is...kindness.
Galatians 5:22

Several months ago when I walked into my local Wal-Mart store, my eye was immediately drawn to a large poster picturing several arrogant girls standing around with some pretty awful scowls on their faces. It was an advertisement of the latest DVD movie being offered for sale. And having my mind on this book and the fruit of the Spirit—and more specifically on "kindness"—I couldn't help but react to the title of the movie: *Mean Girls.*

Now contrast these "mean girls" with my friend Judy who helped me serve at a young woman's bridal shower. I worked kitchen duty while Judy moved among the women asking if they needed anything, patting them on the shoulder, and making sure everyone was comfortable. Graciously Judy chatted with each woman as she carried the heavy silver coffeepot around the room, refilling cups and removing dirty dishes and soiled napkins. Then, even though I was in the kitchen, I heard one guest (a mean girl!) sneer as Judy moved out of earshot, "She's too nice."

Since my encounter with the "mean girls," I've given much thought to those words, "She's too nice." What Judy did for all of us—including an ungrateful woman—was to actively live out kindness, the next fruit of the Spirit. Judy modeled the grace and ministry of kindness not only for those other women, but for me as well. As you'll soon see, the highest compliment a Christian can receive is to be described as "too nice." When people say that of you or me, we can definitely know we are truly exhibiting the Spirit's fruit!

Finding Out More About Kindness

Let's backtrack a minute and review our walk with God. In this section of our book, we're learning about the actions of patience, kindness, and goodness in dealing with the people in our lives. As we face people each day and as we experience any pain they may inflict upon us, we are to be patient, to do nothing. And this response can be achieved only when we ask God to fill us with His patience. Only God can help us do nothing.

But after asking for patience, it's time to make a move, to go into action, to get up and do something! And that "something" is kindness, the next fruit on the Lord's list— "the fruit of the Spirit is...kindness" (Galatians 5:22). And even though the fruit of kindness is borne in our lives as we walk by the Spirit, that walk involves living out several commands given to us in God's Word. Make notes and interact with the scriptures that follow to learn more about kindness.

✎ *A Word from God's Word About Kindness...*

- Ephesians 4:25-32 warns Christians against conduct that grieves the Holy Spirit and hurts the heart of God.[1] You'll want to get well acquainted with these verses for sure! But for now, focus on the commands in verse 32. Paul wraps up his list of meanness—bitterness, wrath, anger, clamor, and evil speaking—and tells us to instead *"be kind...to one another"* (verse 32). The Living Bible simply and bluntly says, *"Stop being mean...[and] instead, be kind to each other."*

- Another call to kindness is in Colossians 3:12. Here God tells us to *"clothe [ourselves] with...kindness."* Kindness is a basic Christian virtue that helps all relationships. Therefore we are to put on kindness—like we put on our clothes—in all our relationships.

- And how are we to act toward those who are not Christians? With kindness! *"The Lord's servant must not quarrel;*

instead, he must be kind to everyone" (2 Timothy 2:24). Kindness is an important element in Christian witnessing. Christians have been known through the ages by their love and concern for others, and that should be our goal too.

Defining Kindness—Kindness "Does Something"

My operating definition of kindness, which helps me immensely in cultivating and showing concern for others, is "kindness plans to do something." While patience does nothing sinful while resisting in patience (see chapter 6), kindness now plans to act.

Kindness, like all the other fruit of the Spirit, desires godly action and, therefore, looks for opportunities to do something. Kindness actively moves out, preparing for the actions of goodness (which we will look at in the next chapter). Kindness actively asks, "Who needs love? How can I ease someone's burden? How can I touch another person?" Kindness is tenderness and concern for other people. It is also a sweetness of disposition and a matter of the heart, "a grace that mellows all that might be harsh."[2]

Cultivating Kindness

The book I turn to each morning during my prayer time contains a sobering prompt that has helped me grow in kindness. It instructs me to pray for "greater love and compassion for others." Well, I have to tell you that whenever I see these words, I am humbled to the core as I examine my heart and soul. This call to prayer always makes me realize how much more I need this godly quality in my life! But prayer and the following aspects of kindness have helped me in this area. Here's what I've discovered.

1. *Caring is a part of kindness*—When you genuinely care about people, you find yourself paying attention to their circumstances and being concerned about their welfare. You get involved in their lives. As your love grows, the details of their lives become more and more important to you. It begins to really matter to you if they are sad or discouraged, struggling or in pain, needy or lonely. (Unfortunately that caring doesn't come nearly as easily for me when it comes to the problem people in my life.)

This is where prayer helps. If you follow Jesus' instruction to "pray for those who mistreat you" (Luke 6:28), radical changes occur in your heart. For starters, prayer causes you to become vitally and spiritually involved in the lives of those you pray for. Also, through prayer, God changes your heart and mind by softening your harshness and melting your selfishness into concern for others...including your enemies. Caring about others eliminates unfriendliness, a lack of compassion, and a judgmental spirit. So ask God to help you have greater love and compassion for others.

2. *Thinking is a part of kindness*—Another sure sign that your concern for people is growing is when you begin to think about others and the conditions of their lives. When

you find yourself looking at people and thinking, "What would help her? What would help him? What does he need? What does she need?" When you ask God, "How can I serve this person? How can I make his or her life easier? How can I touch her life and lift her burden?"

As we're learning, kindness plans to do something, and that takes a certain amount of thought and prayer. King David models this for us. When he became the king of Israel, David asked, "Is there anyone still left of the house of Saul [the previous king] to whom I can show kindness?" (2 Samuel 9:1). You see, David was *thinking* about showing kindness to the heirs of the former king. Can you think of someone you can be kind to?

To grow in kindness, ask God to give you a caring heart and a creative mind. Begin looking around to see the needs of people in your home, your neighborhood, your workplace, and your church. Hurting people are literally everywhere! One shocking statistic reports, "Ninety percent of all mental illness…could have been prevented, or could yet be cured, by simple kindness."[3] What can you think of doing today that would touch another life with kindness?

3. *Noticing is a part of kindness*—Another way to practice kindness is to notice other people's needs. All you have to do is use your God-given capacity for observation. As the Bible says, "Ears that hear and eyes that see—the Lord has made them both" (Proverbs 20:12). You can *always* be watching and listening to those around us. In fact, this is one of the ways God cares for us: "The eyes of the Lord are on the righteous and his ears are attentive to their

prayer" (1 Peter 3:12). And you can care for people in the same way God cares for you...just by paying attention and being on the lookout for people's needs.

I read this story about an evangelist's mom who practiced this sort of kindness and observation. One day he found her sitting at the table with an elderly homeless man. Apparently she had gone shopping, met the needy man along the way, and provided a warm meal for him. During their conversation the homeless man said, "I wish there were more people like you in the world." That's when his mom replied, "Oh, there are! But you must just look for them." The old man simply shook his head, saying, "But lady, I didn't need to look for you. You looked for me!"[4] Take note—when you begin to notice others, you'll soon know their wants and needs just as this kind woman did.

And here's another story about a woman who walks in kindness. It's about "a Hawaiian woman who strings a number of leis early each Sunday morning, not for anyone in particular! Then she goes to church praying, 'Lord, who needs my leis today? A newcomer? Someone discouraged. Lead me to the right people.'"[5]

These stories show us two pictures of kindness—two real women filled with God's love who go out actively looking for those in need. Two women who, in kindness, plan to do something, then keep a keen eye out and notice others.

Pray to grow in God's grace of kindness. Constantly ask God to work in your heart to help you care, think, and notice the people He places in your life. Look to God for His help with unkind emotions and thoughts about others. Then obey God's commands for kindness.

Heart Response

In our culture today, and in places like your school and even at home, being too nice may not sound very cool. But that's exactly what kindness is! Those around you may be "mean," but God is asking you to be kind.

When the book of Galatians was written—the book where the fruit of the Spirit is listed—the common slave name *chrestos* came from the same Greek root word for kindness. The first-century pagans confused *chrestos* (slave) with the word *Christos* for Christ and began calling Christians by a nickname that meant "goody-goody."[6] That's the same as being "too nice." The spelling of these two Greek words varies by just one letter, and they are amazingly similar! When you walk with God and copy Jesus, you too will be kind. You'll be "too nice"!

My friend Judy was spoken of as being "too nice." Why? Because she was kind. Because she was serving as a *chrestos*, a slave. Because she was caring, thinking, noticing, and touching. And because she is a *Christos*, a kind of Christ, a "goody-goody," Judy's kindness should be a goal for you as well.

Things to Do Today to Walk in Kindness

1. Pray every day this week for God to fill your heart with His compassion. Then write out how praying for compassion made a difference in you and in your week.

2.   Live out God's command to be kind to others at home (Ephesians 4:32). Remember, what you are at home is what you are. Think of ways to help out your parents and your brothers and sisters, even your grandparents. Make it your goal to make their lives easier. What can—and will—you do today?

3.   Pray for your enemies—those people who mistreat and use you (Luke 6:28). You will find you cannot hate a person you are praying for. You also can't neglect that person. Try it! You'll find it's true.

4.   List several ways you can show God's kindness to your Number One problem person. Remember this thought—Kindness is the ability to love people more than they deserve.

*Would You Like to Know More
About Kindness?
Check It Out!*

✓ Read 2 Samuel 9:1-7. What question did David ask when he became king of Israel (verse 1)?

What did he do or what actions of kindness did he take when his question was answered (verses 2-7)?

✓ Read 2 Kings 4:8-10. To whom and how did the Shunammite woman show kindness?

✓ Read Acts 9:36. Describe Dorcas' many acts of kindness. What did she do for the widows in her community (verse 39)?

✓ Read Luke 9:12-13. For whom was Jesus concerned?

Contrast Jesus' actions and concerns with the disciples' behavior.

✓ What do these four examples reveal about how you show—or don't show—kindness?

8

A Time to Do Everything

The fruit of the Spirit is...goodness.
Galatians 5:22

Late one evening I crawled into bed clutching a book, hoping I could stay awake to read at least five minutes before turning out the lamp. It had been another wild and full day (you know, like the ones you have too!). I had just about had it...but I was going to give the five minutes a try anyway. The book in my hand was a treasure I had found that morning at the bookstore, and all day long I had been relishing the thought of opening this small delight. Only one copy was on the shelf at the store, and its title had caught my eye and captured my attention—*People Whose Faith Got Them into Trouble*.[1] Finally it was time—if I could just stay awake! As

I began reading this book subtitled "Stories of Costly Discipleship," the opening words of the first chapter caught my attention so completely that I read much longer than usual. Here's what I read:

> The sound of hooves at midnight—horsemen galloping into the courtyard—and the clatter of armor as soldiers surround the house wake the old man. Two officers dismount and pound on the wooden door with the butt ends of their spears. Maids in disheveled nightclothes rush upstairs and urge the white-haired fugitive to hide under the bed, in a closet...anywhere. Instead, he hushes them, drapes a cloak over his frail shoulders, descends the stairs, opens the door and invites the men who have come to arrest him inside.
>
> He instructs the maids, "Quickly, prepare hot food and something to drink. Can't you see these men have ridden hard tonight? They need refreshment; give them the best in the house."
>
> Confused by this unexpected reception, the arresting officers crowd into the room and cluster around a bronze charcoal brazier on the floor. As they warm their numb hands against the cold night of February 22, 166, Polycarp, elderly bishop of Smyrna...makes every effort to see that his guests are comfortable. He personally serves the officers and soldiers alike from the warm dishes his maids have prepared.[2]

What a powerful example of Christian goodness! A man being hunted down, a man who would soon taste death by execution at a fiery stake, was showing love to his persecutors! This man was exhibiting the Spirit's fruit:

> —*patience* allowed him to graciously receive his captors,
>
> —*kindness* thought of their needs, and then
>
> —*goodness* followed through.

Serving them himself, the man being led to death met the needs of those leading him. This story of Polycarp offers us a vivid example of the fruit of the Spirit in action.

Reviewing Our Progress

Do you realize that just as a garden is laid out by a plan, God designs your life according to a plan? He uses the people, events, and circumstances of our lives to guide us along the path toward godliness. And He leads us step by step. Truly, He knows how to grow us to be like Him!

And speaking of gardens and growing, I was thinking about these three fruit of the Spirit that help us get along with everybody—patience, kindness, and goodness. My thoughts went something like this...

> *Patience* is like a seed hidden beneath the surface. It silently waits in the dark earth, hidden from view, doing nothing (it seems!), while it secretly, quietly, and slowly incubates life. This

sweet fruit makes it possible for kindness and goodness to develop.

Kindness grows from the seed of patience in the dark depths where it develops a root system. Kindness pushes its head up through the soil, wanting to break forth and do something until, at last, it cracks through the soil, visible to all.

Goodness blossoms forth, along with its works of love blessing all who see it...which is what this luscious fruit of the Spirit is all about!

Getting a Handle on Goodness

Getting God's fruit of goodness into your life will be easier when you understand three things. These truths will help you in your conduct toward others.

1. *Goodness is spiritual in its origin*—The Bible shows us that God is good (Psalm 33:5; Nehemiah 9:25,35). From cover to cover, the Bible tells the story of God's gracious goodness. One scholar defines this goodness as "the sum of all God's attributes...express[ing] the...excellence of the divine character."[3] And yet, as God's children, we can exhibit His goodness.

2. *Goodness is active*—While kindness plans to do something good for others, goodness moves into total action. God *in* us and His presence *with* us produces *His* goodness in

us. And His goodness in us then results in kind deeds that benefit others.

3. *Goodness is a readiness to do good*—Goodness is also completely dedicated to helping others live well.[4] It is a readiness to do good,[5] up on tip-toe, ready and waiting to do good to others.

I'm sure you agree that your family and friends, your church and school—even the whole world!—need people who are actively kind. People who walk out their doors every day ready to do good—not just think about it or pray about it, but really do it. People who are devoted to making the lives of others better.

Defining Goodness

As I tried to understand goodness, it helped me to understand it as *goodness does everything!* In other words, it does everything it can to shower God's goodness upon others. Goodness follows through on the wonderful thoughts of kindness. Goodness takes the giant step from good intentions to actually doing everything it can to serve others. John Wesley, the famous preacher of several centuries ago, understood this principle of doing everything. In fact, he made it a rule for his life and put it in these words:

> Do all the good you can,
> by all the means you can,
> in all the ways you can,
> in all the places you can,

at all the times you can,
to all the people you can,
as long as ever you can.

Finding Out More About Goodness

How does God's goodness in us work itself out? It's pen time again! Make notes as you let these scriptures work in your heart.

✎ *A Word from God's Word About Goodness...*

- First there is the matter of your walk with God. You are called by God to

  —"*walk in love*" (Ephesians 5:2),

  —"*walk in Him*" (Colossians 2:6),

  —"*walk in a manner worthy of the God who calls you*" (1 Thessalonians 2:12),

  —"*walk in the same manner as Jesus walked*" (1 John 2:6), and

  —"*walk by the Spirit*" (Galatians 5:16).

- A life characterized by God's goodness *is* walking by the Spirit! Through this kind of living you can

  — "*overcome evil with good*" (Romans 12:21), and

  —not return "*evil for evil or reviling for reviling, but on the contrary blessing*" (1 Peter 3:9 NKJV).

- Any goodness borne in us is God's. As the Bible says in Romans 3:12, *"There is no one who does good, not even one."* However, as we practice obedience to God's commands, He produces His fruit of goodness in us—fruit which is by His grace and glorifies Him.

Choosing Goodness

Some of the young women in my Bible class realized that to walk with God they had to make some serious choices. Susan, for instance, was hurt by people in her school who were not Christians and who openly despised her for being one. She told me her plan of action: "I've set a goal. No matter what others at school do or say to me, I have decided I'm going to respond in goodness and be a good advertisement for Christ. And it's already working!"

Ann, too, was hurt—but by the Christians in her youth group at church. What did she do? How did she handle this? "I chose to not feel hurt when I was not invited to join them in their activities. I chose to not feel bitterness or resentment. I just need to show my love for them."

And then there is Maria. She faces a hostile, persecuting boss at her part-time job, a person she described as mean and rude. Her situation at work boiled down to a spiritual decision for her. She could react in the wrong way...or she could respond in the right way, God's way. She wrote, "I had to make a choice—give back what he is dishing out or show him the kindness and goodness of the Lord."

Examples like these could go on and on, and choices like these go on and on too. But I'm sure you're getting a picture about how to walk in goodness from these girls who are just like you. Like these young women, your walk with God requires many decisions on your part as you constantly look to God and ask Him, "What is the right thing to do?"

Walking in Goodness

Yes, walking with God (which is what this book is all about) requires that you and I make serious choices. As one fellow traveler notes, "The Spirit life includes goodness, and goodness doesn't come naturally; it always requires a decision."[6] And our relationships with others, especially with those who hurt us, call for choices. For instance, one definite choice we can make when we're hurt by someone is to walk in patience and do nothing. That gives us time to seek to do the right thing. Then, having made the choice not to blow up, not tell someone off, not to succumb to anger, not to fight back, not to take revenge, we can move to the next choice—the choice of kindness—and *plan to do something*, plan to do deeds of kindness.

This choice, my friend, is the focus of our constant battle between the flesh and the Spirit (Galatians 5:17). And it is this kind of choice that keeps you walking with God...even when provoked or hurt or confused by the treatment of others. You and I must put forth the effort of making the right choices—God's choices. And we must turn to God for His help in winning the victory over sin. Then, miracle of miracles, our lives bring glory to Him as His fruit grows and displays itself in our walk with Him!

As you and I walk through the day-in, day-out routines and responsibilities of life, we have many chances to choose goodness, especially as women. Read on—with pen in hand!—and see for yourself God's plan for goodness in your life.

✎ *A Word from God's Word About Goodness...*

- *God's women are to learn goodness.* In Titus 2:5 we read that the young women are taught by other women and encouraged by them to *be good* (Titus 2:5 NKJV).

- *God's women are to be devoted to goodness.* In 1 Timothy 5:10 (NKJV) women are urged to live a life that earns them a reputation *for good works,* to be devoted to *every good work.* And don't forget—your goodness begins at home with the people who live under your roof as well.

- *God's women are to adorn themselves with goodness.* In 1 Timothy 2:10 women are instructed to adorn themselves *with good deeds, appropriate for women who profess to worship God.* One scholar writes that good works "create that spiritual adornment which is the real glory of the Christian woman."[7] Good works indicate a life of selfless devotion to others, an adornment that lies not in what she puts on, but in the loving service she gives out.[8] Clearly God wants our good works to be our chief attraction. Our good works are what He wants others to notice—not our clothes and not our jewelry and not our looks. Our good works reflect our walk with God.

Heart Response

Oswald Chambers, a great saint from years past, writes this about goodness: "Christian character is not expressed by good doing, but by God-likeness. It is not sufficient to do good, to do the right thing. We must have our goodness stamped by the image and superscription of God. It is supernatural all through."[9] In other words, our goal is to grow in godliness, not just to crank out works. As you read through the "Things to Do Today" list that follows, keep in mind that in order to think about others, you must first stop thinking about yourself!

Things to Do Today to Walk in Goodness

1. Confess any thoughts or acts that are not kind or good. Augustine wrote, "The confession of evil works is the first beginning of good works."[10]

2. Take the initiative in meeting the specific needs of others. Remember, "Love means action."[11]

3. Forget your own comfort. "When God is at work in the believer, he desires to be good and to do good....It becomes clear that the good life is not comfort, but godliness."[12]

4. Actively seek to promote the happiness of others—someone in your family, a friend, a co-worker, or a teacher at school. "Kindness is a sincere desire for the happiness of others; goodness is the activity calculated to advance their happiness."[13]

Would You Like to Know More About Goodness?
Check It Out!

✓ What do these verses say about doing good?

Luke 6:27-28—

Romans 2:7—

Romans 2:10—

Romans 12:21—

Galatians 6:10—

✓ Which of these verses were your favorites or the most challenging, and why?

✓ What actions did the following women take that modeled goodness—the desire to do something?

Rebekah in Genesis 24:15-20—

The Shunammite woman in 2 Kings 4:8-10—

Martha and Mary in Luke 10:38 and John 12:2—

Dorcas in Acts 9:36—

Lydia in Acts 16:15—

✓ Which of these women and their acts of goodness inspires you most to minister goodness to others, and why?

9

Looking at Jesus' Actions

Jesus, our wonderful Master and Teacher, perfectly lived out patience, kindness, and goodness. Do you remember Jesus praying in the Garden of Gethsemane? It was time for Him to die, yet He didn't rebel, panic, turn, or fall apart. Instead, He turned to His Father in prayer. Then, after a time of heartfelt and intense prayer, He rose up from the ground filled with God's love, joy, and peace—the first three fruit we studied. Strengthened after His time of prayer and thoroughly prepared, Jesus gathered His sleeping disciples and boldly walked through the garden gate...

...to face people. Jesus knew they were waiting on the other side of the gate. Exactly who was waiting for Jesus outside the garden?

The Traitor

As Jesus confidently walked toward the garden entrance, He said, "Rise, let us go! Here comes my betrayer!" (Matthew 26:46). Jesus definitely knew *what* was about to happen—and He also knew *who* was playing a role in the process. It was Judas! How Christ's heart must have ached as He looked into the face and eyes of a trusted friend. Who was Judas?

—He was one of the 12 men—the 12 disciples—chosen to help Jesus with His ministry of teaching, leading, providing for the needs of others, and working miracles.

—He was one who had been prayed for by the Savior and fed by His miraculous multiplication of loaves and fishes.

—He was one whose dirty feet had been washed by the Savior's holy hands.

—He was one who had heard the words of life and truths about God from the mouth of God Himself.

—He was the one to whom Jesus had entrusted the group's money.

—He was one of the few people who had the privileges he enjoyed on a daily basis in the presence of Jesus.

Yes, there Judas stood, filled with the darkness of hell itself and the evil of Satan. Judas—betrayer. What grief and disappointment must have filled our Lord! Judas, a friend, a disciple, an intimate companion—and now a traitor!

The Mob

And Judas was not alone. He was accompanied by "a great multitude with swords and clubs, from the chief priests and elders of the people" (Matthew 26:47). Included in this group were the officers of the temple (Luke 22:52), a company of Roman soldiers, the chief priests and elders.

Yes, Jesus had to deal with people—as many as a thousand! People who were not very nice. People who were mean and evil. For the next 18 hours, He would face a host of hostile people—people who would abuse Him physically and verbally, people who would hurl insults at Him, along with fists, whips, staves, hammers, and spears. Still to come were the high priest, Caiaphas, the scribes, the elders, and the Council of the Sanhedrin (Matthew 26:57-60).

And there would be even more! The list of Jesus' enemies continues:

- Pilate—who would call for Jesus' death (Matthew 27:2).

- The soldiers—who would strip Him, mock Him, spit on Him, and beat Him (verses 28-30).

- The two thieves crucified with Him—one of whom would insult Him (Luke 23:39-41).

- The crowd—which would hurl abuses and wag their heads in mockery (Matthew 27:39-40).

- The disciples—who would flee, leaving Jesus even more alone (Matthew 26:56).

Truly, the forces of evil had gathered for the purpose of arresting Jesus and putting Him to death.

The Fleshly Response

As soon as Judas kissed Jesus, His enemies came and laid hands on Him and seized Him (Matthew 26:50). In the seconds that followed, we see (again!) the fleshly response of Jesus' disciples in sharp contrast to His gracious response of patience, kindness, and goodness.

Think for a minute about this troubling scene of Jesus' arrest. It happened under the dark cover of night. Possibly a thousand people were involved. There was confusion and panic. Emotions ran high as the Savior of the world met its evil head on.

And in the heat of those emotions, "one of those who were with Jesus reached and drew out his sword, and struck the slave of the high priest, and cut off his ear" (verse 51). We learn from the book of John that this "one" is Peter (John 18:10). Peter showed no patience. Instead, he went into action. He grabbed a sword and swung. No graciousness was exhibited in Peter's desire to slash 'em, dash 'em, thrash 'em, and kill 'em! He also showed no kindness—the kindness of God that desires the best for others.

Peter's action caused someone to suffer. And he certainly showed no goodness—that fruit of the Spirit that does everything for the good of others. Instead, Peter hurt someone in his efforts to protect his Master. Peter most definitely responded in the fleshly way. He chose the easy response. He reacted. He evidenced "the acts of the sinful nature" (Galatians 5:19).

The Godly Response

Jesus also went into action. Notice how His response exhibited the fruit of the Spirit.

The godly response of patience—First, Jesus lived out God's perfect patience. Do you remember our definition of patience in chapter 6? Patience is endurance when injured by others, it is interested in their good, it is without vengeance, and it *does nothing.* Jesus lived every aspect of this gracious fruit. Wanting nothing done in revenge or reaction, He told Peter, "Put your sword back in its place" (Matthew 26:52). Although Jesus definitely could have avenged Himself, He rebuked Peter's puny action by asking, "Do you think I cannot call on my Father, and he will at once put at my disposal more than twelve legions of angels?" (verse 53). Instead of calling on 72,000 angels, Jesus acted in perfect patience. He did nothing and consequently was led away (verse 57) as a lamb to the slaughter (Isaiah 53:7).

The godly response of kindness—And why did Jesus let Himself be led away? Partly because of His kindness. God's kindness is concerned for the welfare of others (even one's enemies). It also desires to better their lives. And it consciously *plans to do something* for them. In kindness, Jesus had "resolutely set out for Jerusalem" (Luke 9:51) in the first place. In kindness, He had also agonized in prayer those three long hours. And now, acting in kindness, he met the mob head on instead of fleeing. In His divine kindness, Jesus planned to do something for His enemies. He planned to die for them!

The godly response of goodness—Finally, in goodness, our Jesus moved into action. Goodness is active kindness and flows out of a heart that stands ready to do good. And goodness *does everything possible* to help others live well.

So what did Jesus do? He turned to the man whose ear Peter had cut off, "touched the man's ear and healed him" (Luke 22:51). This man was one of the enemy mob. He had come to arrest Jesus, yet now he found himself on the receiving end of Jesus' goodness. He experienced a miracle of goodness. In fact, his healing was the last service Jesus rendered before being bound. Appropriately for our Savior and Lord, "the last action of that hand, while it was still free, was one of love, one of rendering service to men."[1]

Heart Response

Truly Jesus is the God of all grace who is "able to make all grace abound to you, so that in all things at all times, having all that you need, you will abound in every good work" (2 Corinthians 9:8)! Having seen our Savior's great graciousness in terrible circumstances, how can we ever again lash out at others? How could we ever again be impatient with others after witnessing the beauty and grace of our Lord's patience with His killers? How could we ever again wish evil or ill upon others after watching our Savior's kindness as He walked the lonely road to Jerusalem to die for us all? And how could we ever again strike out physically or verbally at another after seeing our Savior's healing touch for an enemy?

Becoming more like Jesus requires us to be filled with God's grace—His Spirit's gifts of patience, kindness, and goodness. To respond in His way requires looking to Him to "find grace to help us in our time of need" (Hebrews 4:16). Let's look to Him now in prayer...

It is in prayer, dear Father,
    that we thank You for the people in our lives
    who cause us to need Your grace so.
We acknowledge that
    Your patience,
    Your kindness, and
    Your goodness enable us
        to do nothing harmful,
        to truly care, and
        to act out Your love toward others.
In our pain...our tears...our suffering...
    we look to You, O heart of love.
May we refuse to act or react until we have again
    looked at our Savior's actions and
    seen His patience...His kindness...His
    goodness.
May we grow in these graces.
In Jesus' name,
    who came not to be ministered to but to
    minister to others...even to the point of
    giving His life as a ransom. Amen.

Things to Do Today to Grow More Like Jesus

1. Read again Matthew 26:36-46. List three or four things these verses teach you about preparing to associate and to interact with people. Start carrying the list around with you. Put it on your prayer list too!

2. What are some of the ways you have responded in the past to people who have caused you pain—who were critical of you, or made fun of you, or snubbed you, or hurt you? What is your usual way of responding to such people?

3. After learning about Jesus' actions of goodness toward unkind people, how will you respond the next time you are mistreated? How will you...

   ...resist in patience?

   ...plan for kindness?

   ...give in goodness?

Would You Like To Know More About Growing Like Jesus? Check It Out!

✓ Read Matthew 26:47-68 and 27:27-44. Make a list of the people or groups of people Jesus faced. Then, across from each, list the different ways these people treated Jesus.

<u>People or group</u>   <u>Treatment</u>

✓ What could Jesus have done to defend Himself (Matthew 26:53)?

What did Jesus do instead according to 1 Peter 2:23?

What lessons can you take to heart from Jesus' conduct on that horrible night?

✓ Read again Matthew 26:51-54 and 69-75. By contrast to Jesus' behavior, write out a brief summary of Peter's fleshly behavior.

What lessons can you take to heart from Peter's conduct on that horrible night?

Getting Your
Act Together

10

A Choice to Just Do It

The fruit of the Spirit is...faithfulness.
Galatians 5:22

One day while I was filing some of my husband's papers, a newspaper cartoon fell out of a manila folder. It was an old Pogo strip. And there was Pogo Possum, wearing a colonial general's hat made out of paper, holding a tiny wooden sword, and standing in a George Washington pose on top of a rock. Out of Pogo's mouth came the bubble with these famous words, "We have met the enemy—and they is us!"

"We have met the enemy—and they is us" is exactly how I feel many nights at the end of another day that began with good intentions. The discouragement comes when I realize that I, too, chose to watch the national average of 6.4 hours of TV...that I chose to eat the foods that generally move people to the "20 pounds overweight" category...that I've hardly touched the "to do" list (I can't even find it!)...or that I have failed to open my Bible. I am truly my own worst enemy when it comes to being a disciplined woman. How greatly I need the Spirit's fruit of faithfulness and self-control!

Taking Time to Review

Before we step into this final section of this book, I want us to think again about our progress. On our journey to discover the meaning of each fruit of the Spirit listed in Galatians 5:22-23, we first learned about love and joy and peace—attitudes that bloom with great sacrifice.

Next we dealt with the challenge of handling people God's way—and the way Jesus did—by looking to the Holy Spirit for His patience, kindness, and goodness.

And now it's time to move on to conquer the discipline of self. If you're cringing at the very thought, rejoice... and relax! There's hope! Faithfulness, gentleness, and self-control are grace gifts from God that make it possible for you to triumph over weakness, impulsiveness, and laziness. When you walk by the Spirit you win over procrastination, stubbornness, and unhealthy desires. So hang on! It may be a rough road to walk, but a pattern for victory through God's Spirit awaits you at the other end.

Now, first on God's list for getting your act together is faithfulness.

Finding Out More About Faithfulness

As Christians, God's faithfulness is to be part of our character. And faithfulness is critical because, as someone has said, "The final criterion God will use to judge us will not be success but faithfulness."[1] The following insights will help you to understand faithfulness and how better to walk in it.

Insight #1: The God of faithfulness—From the first page of the Bible to the last, we see God's faithfulness. First, we learn that God is faithful. The psalmist declared, "I will make your faithfulness known through all generations" (Psalm 89:1). Moses did that when he praised God, exulting, "He is the Rock!...a faithful God" (Deuteronomy 32:4). And here's a thought for you: One scholar reached this conclusion—"God is a Rock...and there should be something of the rock in us."[2]

Second, the New Testament shows us that Jesus is faithful. His very name is "Faithful and True" (Revelation 19:11). His ultimate demonstration of faithfulness is this: Because Jesus was faithful, He "made himself nothing, taking the very nature of a servant, being made in human likeness. And being found in appearance as a man, he humbled himself and became obedient to death—even death on a cross! (Philippians 2:7-8)."[3]

And here's something else we learn—God's Word is faithful. The apostle John was told to write down his visions because "these words are trustworthy and true" (Revelation 21:5). We are blessed to experience the faithfulness of the Godhead *and* the Bible!

Insight #2: The core of faithfulness—Faithfulness is defined as loyalty, trustworthiness, or steadfastness. It is characteristic of the person who is reliable, and it includes our faithfulness to God and His will, to God and His Word, as well as our loyalty to others. And it also means faithful not only in deed, but also in word.

Insight #3: The marks of faithfulness—What does faithfulness do? What does faithfulness in action look like? Well, if you were watching a woman who is walking with God by His Spirit, you would note these marks:

- She follows through...on whatever she has to do.

- She comes through...no matter what.

- She delivers the goods...whether a returned item or a school paper.

- She shows up...even early so others won't worry.

- She keeps her word...her *yes* means *yes* and her *no* means *no* (James 5:12).

- She keeps her commitments and appointments...you won't find her canceling.

- She successfully transacts business...carrying out any instructions given to her.

- She is regular at church...and doesn't neglect worship.

- She is devoted to duty...just as Jesus was when He came to do His Father's will (John 4:34).

Insight #4: The opposites of faithfulness—We can learn a lot from opposites. For instance, one of those opposites is *fickle.* You've met people who change—change their minds, change their loyalties, change their standards. Nothing seems to matter or be that important. Nothing seems to rate an authentic commitment.

Another opposite of faithful is *unreliable.* An unreliable person doesn't come through, can't be depended on, and can't be trusted with information or responsibility. As the saying goes, you may depend on the Lord—but may He depend on you?

Defining Faithfulness—Faithfulness Means "Do It!"

As I thought about faithfulness, I chose as my own definition the slogan *"Do it!"* or, to quote the Nike shoe ads, *"Just do it!"* Faithfulness means doing it...no matter what. Doing it regardless of feelings, moods, or desires—if the Lord wills (James 4:15).

"Do it!" has become my battle cry as I struggle each day with my special areas of weakness. Tiredness heads the list...followed closely by laziness. But when I make a decision to *do it* and look to God for His strength and purpose in *doing it,* He gives me the grace to have victory over both. We'll look later at more of the enemies of faithfulness, but for now let the motto *"Do it!"* move you toward greater faithfulness. Try it...for an hour, a day, a week. I think you'll amaze yourself (and others!) as they see this sturdy fruit grow in your life through the work of God's faithful Spirit.

And there's nothing like the Scriptures to help you grow! Is your pen nearby? Grab it now and make notes about how each of these verses can help you get your act together concerning faithfulness.

✎ *A Word from God's Word About Faithfulness...*

- Lamentations 3:22-23—*"Because of the LORD's great love we are not consumed, for his compassions never fail. They are new every morning; great is your faithfulness."*

- Romans 3:3—*"What if some did not have faith? Will their lack of faith nullify God's faithfulness?"*

- Revelation 19:11—*"I saw heaven standing open and there before me was a white horse, whose rider is called Faithful and True. With justice he judges and makes war."*

- Revelation 21:5 and 22:6—*"He who was seated on the throne said, 'I am making everything new!' Then he said, 'Write this down, for these words are trustworthy and true....' The angel said to me, 'These words are trustworthy and true. The Lord, the God of the spirits of the prophets, sent his angel to show his servants the things that must soon take place.'"*

- 1 Corinthians 4:2—*"Now it is required that those who have been given a trust must prove faithful."*

Realizing the Need for Faithfulness

Boy, is there ever a need for faithfulness! We women, whether older or younger, have many—*many!*—assignments from God, and there's no way to accomplish them without faithfulness. Faithful diligence and discipline is needed every step of the way...and throughout the day. For instance...

Homework—Like you, I have "schoolwork" and papers to turn in as I work daily to meet my writing deadlines and turn in my book manuscripts...on top of taking care of a household—both the people and the place. My work at my desk really forces me to follow my maxim *"Do it."* I call it "the discipline of the desk" and mentally chain myself there each day to get my work done, to meet my commitments, to come through on time, to turn in my homework! I like what the great British statesman Winston Churchill said about doing his writing, his "homework." He wrote, "Shut yourself in your study...and make yourself write. Prod yourself!—kick yourself!—it's the only way."[4] That's another way of saying "Do it!" when it comes to the desk.

Devotions—I'm sure you desire the mark of God's freshness on your life. And how is that achieved? By faithfully going to God's Word on a day-by-day basis. Just as a flower needs water to flourish, so we need to drink daily from God's living Word.

Friends—You need to be a faithful friend, but first you must be sure you have the right kind of friends—friends who know and love Jesus Christ. Then be faithful to them, stand with them as together you face the challenges of school...and even the persecution that may come with your belief. And for those friends and acquaintances who don't yet know Jesus, be kind and friendly...and faithful to share Him with them.

Church—God expects you to be faithful in the church. For starters, faithful attendance promotes your spiritual growth. Church is also where you serve God's people, which calls for faithfulness.

William Carey, the father of modern missions, was faithful in his service to God in India for 41 years! When he was asked what his secret to success as a missionary was, he replied, "I can plod; I can persevere in any definite pursuit. To this I owe everything."[5] You affect the world when you are faithful to just faithfully plod on in whatever work God has called you to do!

Struggling to Be Faithful

There's no doubt that to be faithful is a natural, fleshly struggle. That's why we so need to choose to look to God for His strength! Every day we are tempted to do nothing... or as little as possible. Every day we struggle with excuses and challenges like these:

- *Tiredness*...says, "I can't do it." Tiredness moans, "I can't get up...I can't get up and catch the bus...I can't make it to church...I can't study...I'm just too tired!"

- *Laziness*...says, "I don't want to do it." Laziness whines, "I don't want to do my work chores...I don't want to get up and check on my little brother...I don't want to sign up for a ministry...I don't want to go to Bible study."

- *Hopelessness*...says, "It doesn't matter if I do it." Hopelessness asks, "Why try?" and then gives up. Hopelessness easily comes to the erroneous conclusion that "it doesn't matter if I do it."

- *Procrastination*...kills faithfulness with its attitude "I'll do it later." Procrastination announces, "I'll prepare for that class later...I'll finish my homework later...I'll clean up my room later...I'll call the members of my study group later." And exactly what do we think will happen later? Do we really think the frenzy of life will slow down, that some magical minutes will miraculously open up, that new energy will mysteriously arrive, and we'll feel like doing the task we're putting off?

- *Rationalization*...is a subtle but evil perspective on life and responsibility. Rationalization says, "Someone else will do it." Rationalization calculates, "Someone else will set up for the meeting... Someone else will make the announcement...Someone else will get ready for the group."

- *Apathy*...says, "I don't care if I do it." Apathy shrugs, "I don't care if the dishes get done...I don't care if I'm a good daughter or sister or student...I don't care if I read my Bible...I don't care if I grow...I don't care if I'm faithful."

- *Rebellion*...is the attitude that should frighten us most. Rebellion says, "I won't do it." Rebellion stubbornly states, "I won't do what the Bible says...I won't help out at home...I won't do what my parents ask...I won't do what the counselor advised." Rebellion is a hardness that we should fear because, as the Bible teaches, "A man [or woman] who remains stiff-necked...will suddenly be destroyed—without remedy" (Proverbs 29:1). There is no deadlier attitude of the heart than rebellion—whether blatant, outspoken rebellion or quiet rebellion, when you simply and silently go about life in your own way.

Are you wondering where you can get the strength necessary for all this faithfulness? Where you can get the desire? Where you can get much needed help? Well, good news! Our great God ends our struggles by making all we need to be faithful available to us through His grace.

Praise God that you and I can choose to go to Him when we are too tired, too lazy, too uncommitted, too sick, or too sorry for ourselves. We can choose to do as David, the shepherd-king of Israel, did. He "found strength in the LORD his God" (1 Samuel 30:6). David repeatedly declared, "The Lord is the stronghold of my life" (Psalm 27:1). We, too, can find in Him the strength (*His* strength), the vision (*His* vision), and the faithfulness (*His* faithfulness). Indeed, He is waiting to give us His faithfulness.

Heart Response

My friend, faithfulness is such a rarity in this world! Do you realize that if you will walk in faithfulness, you will become a "hero"—one of God's faithful heroes and a hero to others? I close this chapter with the following definition of a "hero." I pray that it will move you to choose to look to God for greater faithfulness!

> The hero does not set out to be one. He is probably more surprised than others by such recognition. He was there when the crisis occurred... and he responded as he always had in any situation. He was simply doing what had to be done! Faithful where he was in his duty there... he was ready when the crisis arose. Being where he was supposed to be...doing what he was supposed to do...responding as was his custom...to circumstances as they developed... devoted to duty—he did the heroic![6]

Things to Do Today to Walk in Faithfulness

1. Choose to call upon God in prayer. David wrote, "When I called, you answered me; you made me bold and stout-hearted" (Psalm 138:3).

2. Choose to be faithful in small things. "Whoever can be trusted with very little can also be trusted with much, and

whoever is dishonest with very little will also be dishonest with much" (Luke 16:10).

3. Choose to rely on God's strength. "I can do everything through him who gives me strength" (Philippians 4:13).

4. Choose to fight self-indulgence. "I beat my body and make it my slave" (1 Corinthians 9:27).

5. Choose to eliminate laziness and idleness. "[She] does not eat the bread of idleness" (Proverbs 31:27).

6. Choose to begin at home. "She watches over the affairs of her household" (Proverbs 31:27).

7. Choose to be faithful in all things. Women must be "trustworthy in everything" (1 Timothy 3:11).

8. Choose to take a quick inventory of your own Christian walk. Then ask God for His strength to go to work on getting His faithfulness into your life...just for today.

Would You Like to Know More
About Faithfulness?
Check It Out!

✓ Read Matthew 25:14-30, Jesus' parable of the talents. What words did Jesus use to praise those who are reliable?

What words did He use regarding those who are not faithful?

What do you find most encouraging from Jesus' story and teaching on faithfulness?

✓ Read 1 Timothy 3:11 and list the four qualities required in a woman who serves in her church.

Why do you think faithfulness is one of the qualifications for service to others in a church?

✓ Read the following verses in your Bible, noting how each instructs you regarding faithfulness and encourages you to be faithful.

Psalm 138:3—

Proverbs 31:27—

Luke 16:10—

1 Corinthians 9:27—

Philippians 4:13—

11

A Choice to Take It

The fruit of the Spirit is...gentleness.
Galatians 5:22-23

Before I began teaching and writing about the fruit of the Spirit, I meditated on gentleness for one whole year! Needless to say, that was one entire year devoted to cultivating gentleness in my own life. Then, as I've continued my study and worked my way through this book, God has given me a second year to think about gentleness.

Here's one thing I've discovered in the process: Of all the blossoms along the path we walk with God, the flower of gentleness appears so fragile, yet as we'll soon see, it develops out of the strongest of underground root systems. So what makes the flower of gentleness bloom?

Finding Out More About Gentleness

As we move toward the finish of our journey toward what it means to walk by the Spirit, remember that to get your act together requires faithfulness. Faithfulness just "does it," whatever "it" is that lies in your path to be done. And to "do it" requires leaning on God and looking to Him for His strength and resolve. And now, with gentleness, we quickly learn that we have to depend again on God.

Exactly what is the fruit of the Spirit called gentleness? Briefly, gentleness...

- means to be gentle or meek, to be lowly or humble,
- is a form of self-control that Christ alone can give,
- expresses itself in a submissive spirit toward both God and man, and
- is the opposite of self-reliant arrogance.

And, as you'll discover, gentleness is truly grown in a hothouse—and there's a high price to pay to cultivate its bloom!

Catching On to the Meaning of Gentleness

Just why is gentleness so costly? And how is it grown in our hearts? Here are a few answers.

1. *Gentleness means trusting the Lord*—By now you definitely know that you must trust the Lord for every fruit of the Spirit—and gentleness is no different. Explaining Jesus'

words, "Blessed are the meek, for they will inherit the earth" (Matthew 5:5), one Bible scholar wrote:

> "The meek" [or gentle] describes the person who is not resentful. He bears no grudge....He finds refuge in the Lord and commits his way entirely to him....Yet *meekness is not weakness*....It is submissiveness under provocation, the willingness rather to *suffer* than to *inflict* injury. The meek [or gentle] person leaves everything in the hand of him who loves and cares.[1]

Did you catch it? Gentleness is *not* resentful, it bears *no* grudge, and it is *not* involved in reflecting on present or past injuries.

So what does the woman characterized by gentleness do instead? She finds refuge in the Lord and His ways. This enables her to endure unkind behavior and suffering in humble submission to an all-wise, caring Father, trusting totally in His love.

Are you wondering, How in the world can anyone bear such bad treatment? For me the answer boils down to one word—faith. No, make that three words—faith in God! The invisible root system of gentleness goes deep into the rich soil of faith. Faith believes that God is able to help us handle everything that happens in our lives. Our faith in the God behind this truth keeps us from struggling and fighting because faith believes God can and will enable us and fight for us (Psalm 60:12).

Now do you see why I've been at work on this fruit for two years? I have the feeling I'll be doing it for many more!

2. *Gentleness means submitting to the Master*—An expert on the Greek language paints this picture of gentleness. He writes, "The adjective gentle...is used of an animal that has been tamed and brought under control."[2] Do you realize...

- the word *tame,* which is the opposite of wild, describes one accustomed to control by another?

- the word *tame* suggests one whose will has been broken or who has allowed himself or herself to be dominated by the will of another?

- the tame person, therefore...

  —has been toned down and exhibits complete dependence on another.

  —has yielded all will to another's control.

  —unquestioningly and humbly obeys what is ordered and accepts what is given.

  —is docile and obedient and pliable, as opposed to fierce.

  —is easy to work with and to be with.[3]

You (and me too!) may not be sure you like what you're reading or what gentleness implies! But it helps to think about meekness in terms of submitting to your Master, the Lord Jesus. Don't you desire to be controlled by Him? Don't you truly yearn for Him to take complete charge of your life?

To lead and guide you? To protect and care for you as you follow Him unquestioningly in faith? Don't you want to be easy to work with and be with?

I think so! So breathe a huge sigh of release and hand over to God any part of your life that you have not yet given to Him. Thank Him—as your Master and as the Master Gardener—that He is able to care for all of you.

3. *Gentleness means following Jesus' example*—I have a confession to make. As the definition of gentleness became clearer...and tougher, I felt more and more hopeless. But when I saw in God's Word that Jesus was gentle, the meaning of gentleness became much clearer and cooler.

Here's how Jesus described Himself. He called out, "Take my yoke upon you and learn from me, for I am gentle and humble in heart" (Matthew 11:29). Do you want to follow Jesus' example of gentleness? Then commit your way to Him. Jesus' gentleness was grounded in a complete trust in His loving Father. And yours can be, too, as you follow His example.

4. *Gentleness means bowing the soul*—The Old Testament gives us a lovely word picture that helped me with gentleness. Visualize this: The Old Testament term for gentleness (*anab*)[4] describes a mature, ripened shock of grain with its head bent low and bowed down. Just think about it. As wheat grows, the young sprouts rise above the rest. Their heads shoot up the highest because no grain has yet formed. In their immaturity little "fruit," if any, has appeared. But as time passes and maturity sets in, fruit develops and grows— so much of it that the heavy stalk bends and its head sinks

lower and lower. And the lower the head bows, the greater the amount of fruit there is on it.

Oh, for us to be this kind of Christian woman—one with a lowered head, seasoned and mature, well past the stages of pride! Oh, if we would only bend in need, bow the soul, and trust in God!

Putting on Gentleness

Gentleness means putting on a gentle spirit. Gentleness demands a choice from us, a choice and a decision to "put on" the clothing of gentleness (1 Peter 3:4). What individual garments make up the wardrobe of gentleness? From 1 Peter 3:1-6 we discover:

—*The garment of submission* (verse 1): All Christians are to submit themselves to others. (Christians are to submit to every human institution in government,[5] servants are to be submissive to their masters with all respect,[6] Christ submitted without a word to His tormentors,[7] and wives are encouraged to be submissive to their own husbands.[8])

—*The garment of pure and reverent behavior* (verses 1-2): This means God-fearing and blameless conduct. It's behavior that refuses to fight, refuses to give in to anger, refuses to think about revenge or payback, and refuses to assert itself.

—*The garment of a gentle and quiet spirit* (verses 3-4): Rather than being obsessed with your outward appearance, the Bible says you—as God's woman—are to focus on your inner condition, the condition of your heart, the "hidden person of the heart." Your aim is a heart that reflects a gentle and quiet spirit. "Gentle" means not causing disturbances, and "quiet" means bearing with tranquility the disturbances caused by others.[9] Only God can give you the strength not to create disturbances, cause a scene, stir up trouble...and not to react to any disturbances created by others.

—*The garment of trust* (verse 5): "The holy women" in the past "put their hope" in God. Theirs was a trust that looked to God in hope and rested in Him.[10] And nothing's changed!

—*The garment of faith* (verse 6): Sarah did not "give way to fear." Like her, you put your faith and trust in God into practice as you graciously accept the details of your life that contribute to a gentle and quiet spirit.

As a woman of God, you are to choose to put on each one of these garments of gentleness—submission, pure and reverent behavior, a gentle and quiet spirit, trust, and faith. Just like you get dressed each day and choose the clothes you put on, you must visit God's wardrobe closet each morning and choose to put on these garments that make for a put-together look—a gentle spirit. God says such a look and such a heart is rare and precious, truly beyond price (verse 4)!

✎ *A Word from God's Word About Gentleness...*

Before you leave the inspection of these garments that are to make up your spiritual wardrobe, read through 1 Peter 3:1-6:

Wives, in the same way be submissive to your husbands so that, if any of them do not believe the word, they may be won over without words by the behavior of their wives, when they see the purity and reverence of your lives. Your beauty should not come from outward adornment, such as braided hair and the wearing of gold jewelry and fine clothes. Instead, it should be that of your inner self, the unfading beauty of a gentle and quiet spirit, which is of great worth in God's sight. For this is the way the holy women of the past who put their hope in God used to make themselves beautiful. They were submissive to their own husbands, like Sarah, who obeyed Abraham and called him her master. You are her daughters if you do what is right and do not give way to fear.

Now note which garments are the hardest for you to put on. Share why. Then share what you are going to do about each necessary garment needed for gentleness in your life.

Are there certain people you refuse to submit to?

Do you fight or get angry with others, say, your parents, brothers or sisters, certain people at school?

Would you say you spend more time on improving your outward looks or your heart?

Do you generally trust in the Lord and rest in Him?

Is it hard for you to, by faith, graciously accept the details of your life?

Defining Gentleness—Gentleness Means "Take It"

My personal definition of the woman who is practicing gentleness or meekness is that she will *take it*. And what is it she takes? Do you remember? She bears with tranquility the disturbances others create. She endures ill treatment. She remains calm in the midst of confusion. Carrying the image of Jesus and His suffering in her mind and heart, she takes it. And this cultivates the fruit of God's gentleness.

I know this can be hard to swallow, and there are obvious moral exceptions (such as physical abuse). And we should always be asking God for His wisdom (James 1:5). But please, open your heart and mind to the beauty of this fruit. God so desires this precious and rare beauty of gentleness to characterize our lives! Hear these thoughts on gentleness:

> Gentleness "is perfect quietness of heart. It is for me to have no trouble; never to be fretted or vexed or irritated or sore or disappointed....It is the fruit of the Lord Jesus Christ's redemptive work on Calvary's cross, manifest in those of His own who are definitely in subjection to the Holy Spirit."[11]

> Gentleness "is...first and chiefly towards God. It is that temper of spirit in which we accept [God's] dealings with us as good, and therefore without disputing or resisting....[It is a humble heart] which...does not fight against

God and... struggle and contend with Him.
This meekness, however, being first of all a
meekness before God, is also such in the
face of men...."[12]

Yes, it's true that in the eyes of others, gentleness may
look like weakness. But producing this fruit calls for the
greatest of strength! Indeed, gentleness has been called
"the fruit of power."[13] And that's the strength and power that
come from looking to God!

As we wrestle with the way to gentleness and how to get
it into our lives, here are some things for you to think and
pray about. Does your life show the fruit of gentleness? Do
you know of any ways or areas you are failing to submit to
God and His management of your life? Do you consider
God's meekness to be weakness? Do you generally bear
grudges toward others or think about revenge? Or are you
mostly able to look beyond any injury caused to you by
someone else...right to the God of wisdom? You may want
to record your first impressions. And you may want to jot
down what you will do to grow in the fruit of gentleness.
In fact, you could do it right here, right now!

Things to Do Today to Walk in Gentleness

1. Trust in God—Trust that, in everything, God knows what He is doing in your life.

2. Pray for gentleness—Prayer develops the gentle habits of bowing, bending, kneeling, yielding, and submitting to God.

3. Refuse to complain and grumble—To complain, one wise believer notes, "is an accusation against God. It questions God's wisdom and God's good judgment. God has always equated complaining with unbelief...[because] to complain is to doubt God. It is the same thing as suggesting that God really doesn't know what He's doing."[14]

4. Refuse to manipulate—Let God resolve your issues for you. Put your faith in scriptures like those in the next section.

Would You Like to Know More About Walking in Gentleness? Check It Out!

✓ What does God command in the following verses?

Galatians 6:1—

Ephesians 4:2—

Colossians 3:12—

1 Timothy 6:11—

2 Timothy 2:24-25—

Titus 3:1-2—

✓ Why is gentleness so important to God?

Why is gentleness so important to your walk with God?

✓ Consider these examples from the Bible of some who learned what it meant to "take it," to look to God for His gentleness in their trying situations.

The apostles—Acts 5:40-41

Stephen—Acts 7:54-60

Paul and Silas—Acts 16:22-25

Servants to both good and harsh masters—1 Peter 2:18-21

✓ What do the following scriptures teach you about trusting God, a key step toward gentleness? And for what can you trust Him?

Psalm 60:12—

Psalm 37:6-7—

Psalm 57:2—

Psalm 138:8—

How will remembering these truths help you "take it"?

12

A Choice to Not Do It

The fruit of the Spirit is...self-control.
Galatians 5:22-23

It was Friday night. Jim and I were sitting in the second row with our two daughters and their college friends. The crowd of thousands who sat in our church were stirring in anticipation. I had heard about the speaker from my first days as a Christian and had also read his classic book *Spiritual Leadership*. And now J. Oswald Sanders was going to speak to us in person! It was one of those once-in-a-lifetime experiences. And I confess! I actually pinched myself to be sure it was real.

As Dr. Sanders mounted the five steps leading up to the pulpit, we held our breaths. That's because this saint of 92 years needed two men to help him get up the stairs. But amazingly, as he finished his greetings and opened his tattered Bible to begin teaching God's Word, strength and vigor came to him. He seemed transformed before us. We were witnessing God's power in the life of a man who had dedicated his many decades to serving and loving the Lord, a man who had walked with God for close to a century.

Do you ever wonder how you can grow to the spiritual stature of a giant like J. Oswald Sanders? I think the answer to that question is more clear when you realize which character quality he placed first in importance for spiritual life and leadership. He named it Number One in his list of "Qualities Essential to Leadership"—Discipline! He writes,

> It has been well said that the future is with the disciplined, and that quality has been placed first in our list, for without it the other gifts, however great, will never reach their maximum potential. Only the disciplined person will rise to his highest powers. He is able to lead because he has conquered himself.[1]

Conquering one's self—self-discipline—is what the Spirit's fruit of self-control is all about. This important gift from God is another key which, when chosen and turned, ignites the power that fuels the fruit of the Spirit. You see, self-control fires up the spiritual energy needed to kindle all of the Christian life. How?

Reviewing God's Fruit

Think about the importance of self-control and the fruit of the Spirit for a moment, beginning with...

...Love, joy, and peace. You can know about love and what it does. And you can have the desire to love. But God's self-control helps you live out that love. The same is true for joy and peace.

...Patience, kindness, and goodness. When every fiber of your flesh wants to be angry and blow up, or circumstances make it hard for you to be kind or good to others, only the Holy Spirit's self-control can help you extend these godly responses.

...Faithfulness and gentleness. By now you know how much of the Spirit's self-control is needed to follow through in faithfulness when laziness and selfishness come so easily. You also know that only God's self-control can give you the strength and gentleness to "take it."

And now for the final fruit on God's list, self-control. And boy, do we need this fruit! It's powerful. It's essential to the Christian life. And it's a rock-solid foundation for our journey to be like Jesus. But how, we wonder, can we ever get a grip on something this large, this important? Answer: It helps to get a grip on what self-control means.

Finding Out More About Self-Control

I love the sweetness of the fruit of the Spirit gentleness and the thought of it being like a soft, beautiful garment we wear when we're walking by the Spirit. However, the spiritual clothing of self-control seems more like armor. Indeed, to practice self-control requires putting on battle gear and getting into a warrior's mentality. You'll see why as you read on.

To begin, the root of "self-discipline" implies the self-restraint of desires and lusts.[2] The famous Greek philosopher Plato used this term to describe the person who has mastered his desires and love of pleasure.[3] Self-control is the controlling power of the will under the operation of the Spirit of God,[4] literally a holding in of one's self with a firm hand by means of the Spirit.[5] In simple terms, self-control is the ability to keep one's self in check.[6]

Did you notice the two repeated topics in these definitions? One is the control of the self—as in *self*-restraint, *self*-government, and *self*-command.[7] The second common thread is the object of control—our passions, appetites, pleasures, desires, and impulses.[8] In other words, all that is physical, sensual, and sexual. Think about it! This includes everything we see, hear, touch, think about, and hunger for. God took pains to list the works of the flesh for us in Galatians 5, among them, immorality, impurity, sensuality, drunkenness, and carousing. Surely no child of God would want to live a life marked by these deeds! But only the Spirit's self-control can help us avoid them.

Gaining Victory Through Self-Control

When you're walking by the Spirit, God's self-control is evident in your life. That's when you reflect these strengths that win victory over sin:

- Self-control controls and checks the self.

- Self-control restrains the self.

- Self-control disciplines and masters the self.

- Self-control holds in and commands the self.

- Self-control says *"No!"* to self.

Here's what a friend of mine did to gain a victory. She wrote this list on a 3" x 5" card and taped it on the bathroom mirror to help her with her problem of overeating. I think her list is a great idea. And you know what? Because the list applies to any and all problems, you might want to make one for yourself. And be sure you put the list in your prayer notebook. These steps will remind you often of God's pattern for self-control.

Defining Self-Control—Self-Control Means "Don't Do It!"

So far in this section about getting your act together, we've learned that faithfulness means—"Do it!" and gentleness means—"Take it!" And now for our understanding, self-control means—"Don't do it!" In times of temptation we are to call on God for His strength and then choose to *don't do it!* In other words, don't give in to emotions, to cravings, to urges. Don't think or do what you know is against God's Word. Don't pamper yourself. Don't make the easy choices. Don't rationalize....And a thousand other "don't do its"! As one pastor explained,

> The word *self-control* means "the ability to say no." It is an evidence of willpower that sometimes expresses itself in "won't power." It is the

ability to say yes at the right time; yes to certain things, and no to others. It is that kind of inward strength that takes all the circumstances and experiences of life and subjects them to evaluation and then decides, "This is right, this is in the will of God," or, "This is wrong, I will put it aside."[9]

God's message to you? Don't do what you could—do what you should!

Struggling for Self-Control

As I was thinking about the struggle for self-control, I made a list of the areas that challenge women—both young and old—most and cause them to need to turn to God for help. (And by the way, these struggles don't go away with age!) It's like a fellow believer observed, "To a greater or lesser degree, if you are alive you are tempted!"[10] That means you (and me too!) need God's self-control every minute of every day in every area of life! Every which way we turn, we face temptation. Therefore we need the Spirit's help to resist in the common areas of life...

Food. Life would definitely be easier if we didn't have to be around food. God created our body to need fuel, but somehow the natural need and desire for food can get out of hand. For instance, because I'm writing about food, my mouth and mind are suddenly yearning to eat something— anything!—but it isn't time to eat. I don't *need* to eat because I just ate lunch. I just *want* to eat! So I'm forcing myself to sit here and keep on writing. I'm thinking, "Elizabeth, just say no. Don't do it. Don't get up and go to the pantry. Fight it. You can have this victory with God's help. Stay seated, keep your mind on the Lord, and work on!"

Now, could I have something to eat? Of course. Would it hurt me to eat? Of course not—well, not now, but maybe in the morning when I got on the scales! But what would the blessings of not giving in to the flesh be? Well, for one thing, I'll make some progress on this chapter as I keep on writing. And here's another—I can have God's victory in this small thing. Plus, by saying no I build a track record with God and gain experience that will help me later when I face a larger thing.

Thoughts. Every woman struggles with her thoughts. You know how easy it is to go into daydream mode and start thinking about things—things that are real or not—such as that cute guy in your English class...and how he did or didn't speak to you. Your thoughts might be innocent enough, but what if they turn into impure thoughts? Or what if you start thinking about the ugly remark someone made about you in the hall between classes? If you're not careful, your thoughts can slide into a state of bitterness and a desire to "get even"...and, well, you know the rest of the scenario all too well!

Money and possessions. These two struggles go hand in hand. Almost every waking minute of every day you're faced with TV ads, billboards, radio commercials, the label on someone's shirt or shoes, all tempting you to desire something and spend your money to get it. And the truth is, most of the stuff being promoted is what you don't need. I'm not saying it's wrong to have nice or cool things. But I am saying this is where self-control comes to your rescue. You have to start telling yourself, "Don't do it! Stop thinking you've just got to have that new and more stylish pair of shoes or jeans!" You need to look to God for His help in curbing yourself, holding yourself back, and controlling your desires. The Spirit can give you the strength to resist the temptation to love the things in the world (1 John 2:15), if you will walk by the Spirit.

Sexual struggles. I've saved this struggle for last, not because it's less important, but because it's vitally important! Maybe your youth pastor has shared the statistics that speak of the sexual activity of even 9- to 12-year-old girls. Sexual purity is an area where you absolutely need God's self-control. Our society tends to overlook and accept sex outside of marriage. In fact, many people expect it! But is this what God wants for His young women? You know the answer—and it's *No!* So how are you going to resist the strong temptation of sexual impurity? This battle, like each of the other struggles we've addressed and along with a lot of other allurements, is won in the same way, my dear young friend. It's fought—and won—when you call upon God, rely on His gift of His self-control, obey Him, and say, *No!* And so it goes. Over and over you look to Him, ask Him for fresh strength and self-control to say again, "Don't do it!" This is the key to winning sexual struggles and cultivating God's self-control in your life.

And now it's pen time! Take a look at these scriptures and

make notes to yourself about how to gain self-control in your areas of struggle.

✎ *A Word from God's Word About Self-Control...*

- For all your battles—The two things you must always remember in your struggle for self-control are:

  — *"Live by the Spirit...[and] you will not gratify the desires of the sinful nature,"* and

  — *"the Spirit...is contrary to the sinful nature"* (Galatians 5:16-17).

- Food—Do you need help? Here's what 1 Corinthians 10:31 says: *"So whether you eat or drink or whatever you do, do it all for the glory of God."*

- Thoughts—Don't give in to sinful thoughts or harmful thought patterns! Instead, *"whatever is true, whatever is noble, whatever is right, whatever is pure, whatever is lovely, whatever is admirable—if anything is excellent or praiseworthy—think about such things"* (Philippians 4:8).

- Money and possessions—Take this advice to heart: *"Do not love the world or anything in the world. If anyone loves the world, the love of the Father is not in him. For everything in the world—the cravings of sinful man, the lust of his eyes and the boasting of what he has and does—comes not from the Father but from the world. The world and its desires pass away, but the man who does the will of God lives forever"* (1 John 2:15-17).

- Sexual struggles—Pay attentions to the do's and don'ts in the Bible!

  —Don't give in! Instead, *"flee from sexual immorality. All other sins a man commits are outside his body, but he who sins sexually sins against his own body. Do you not know that your body is a temple of the Holy Spirit, who is in you, whom you have received from God? You are not your own; you were bought at a price. Therefore honor God with your body"* (1 Corinthians 6:18-20).

  —Do walk by the Spirit! *"It is God's will that you should be sanctified: that you should avoid sexual immorality; that each of you should learn to control his own body in a way that is holy and honorable, not in passionate lust like the heathen, who do not know God"* (1 Thessalonians 4:3-5).

Heart Response

Dear sister, the good news for you and me is that we can claim God's power, walk by His Spirit, exercise self-control, and win the battle over fleshly temptation. Then we will wondrously display the beauty of Christ as we walk with Him through everyday life. We'll truly have our lives together! What a wonderful God we have who makes the storehouse of His grace—His self-control—available to us!

Almost every Christian enjoys the warm but strong exhortations of author and pastor Max Lucado. Here's his encouragement—from his heart to yours—to choose self-control!

I choose self-control...

I am a spiritual being.
After this body is dead, my spirit will soar.
I refuse to let what will rot rule the eternal.
I choose self-control.
I will be impassioned only by my faith.
I will be influenced only by God.
I will be taught only by Christ.
I choose self-control.[11]

—Max Lucado

Now, my friend, may you, too, choose self-control.

Things to Do Today to Walk in Self-Control

1. Begin with Christ. Is He your Lord and Master? Self-mastery begins with being mastered by Christ.

2. Monitor your input. Regulate what you eat, where you go, what you see. Follow David's advice: "I will set before my eyes no vile thing" (Psalm 101:3).

3. Stay busy. Make a schedule...and keep it! Volunteer to help others. Do whatever it takes to stay busy. By doing so, you will refuse to eat "the bread of idleness" (Proverbs 31:27), and you'll find yourself with less time to be tempted.

4. Say "No!" Solomon wrote, "Like a city whose walls are broken down is a man who lacks self-control" (Proverbs 25:28). Echoing that truth is this thought: "The word *No* forms the armament and protective walls of the spiritual city....Sometimes *No* can be a hard word to say, but it is the key to self-control, the word that the Lord blesses."[12]

5. *Pray.* Pray about every aspect of your life! Nothing should be too small to bring before the Lord. Ask for His wisdom to discern good from evil and His strength to say *yes* to the good and *no* to the evil.

Would You Like to Know More About
Walking in Self-Control?
Check It Out!

✓ Look at these scriptures in your Bible and note God's message to you about self-control.

Romans 6:12—

Galatians 5:16—

Romans 6:13—

1 Corinthians 10:31—

Galatians 5:24—

✓ What lessons do you learn from these people about self-control or the lack of self-control?

Joseph and Potiphar's wife—in Genesis 39:7-10.

Moses—Numbers 20:2-11.

Achan—in Joshua 7:21.

David—in 1 Samuel 24:3-7 and 26:7-9.

What reason was behind David's self-control according to 1 Samuel 24:8-15 and 26:10?

David—in 2 Samuel 11:1-4.

13

Looking at Jesus

As we've moved through God's fruit of the Spirit, we have definitely learned more about how to get them into our lives! All along the way Jesus has shown us what each of them looks like lived out by God's grace. And now I want you to look with me at His life again. I want you to look at these final three fruit that deal with the discipline of self—with getting your act together—faithfulness, gentleness, and self-control. As we look at Jesus now, see how many times and in how many ways you witness Him being faithful and "doing it" (like going to the cross), "taking it" (like not talking back), and "not doing it" (like not lashing out or fighting back).

Do you remember when we last observed Jesus? We saw Him arrested and led away for His trial and crucifixion. Do you ever wonder, How did Jesus handle all of this, and what was His mind-set as He faced the cross?

Peter, who watched these awful events unfold, answers these questions for us. Although he denied any tie with Jesus when questioned by others (saying, "I don't know the man!"—Matthew 26:72), Peter continued to follow his Master at a distance. And with a few brief strokes of his pen, Peter summarized our Lord's behavior so that we may follow in His steps, so that we may successfully "do it," "take it," and "don't do it" at the right time and in the right situations. Peter tells us,

> *He committed no sin,*
> *and no deceit was found in his mouth.*
> *When they hurled their insults at him,*
> *he did not retaliate;*
> *when he suffered, he made no threats*
> (1 Peter 2:22-23).

Jesus Committed No Sin

Here's something you should never forget: Throughout His earthly existence—and including His final days—Jesus committed no sin! You've probably had moments when you didn't commit any sin—you know, when all is well and life is good. But let's face it, these times are not the norm.

But now, for a moment, picture the worst of circumstances, the kind Jesus experienced on the way to the cross—the kind packed with betrayal, lying, false charges, unjust punishment, brutality, physical abuse, fists, clubs, rods, whips, nails, and a spear! Then try to imagine committing no sin in that kind of environment! To not sin in such circumstances would definitely be the work of the Holy Spirit. Only He can enable us to walk through difficult situations without sinning!

But why was Jesus suffering? Why was He being so harshly mistreated? All His life He had...

> done well,
> done the right thing,
> done all that God asked and required of
>   Him, and
> successfully carried out the Father's will
>   for His life.

Jesus had...

> taught God's truth,
> healed God's creation,
> fed God's people, and
> taken light into darkness.

Jesus had also...

> preached the gospel to the poor,
> proclaimed freedom for the prisoners,
> restored the sight of the blind, and
> released those who were oppressed (Luke
> 4:18).

Yet Jesus suffered for doing what is right (verse 29). As the holy Son of God, He never in a single instance sinned. He lived His entire life without sin (Hebrews 4:15). Jesus, of all people, did not deserve to suffer in any way!

And here's something else—Even those who condemned Jesus knew He hadn't sinned. He was 100 percent not guilty. For instance, Pilate told the chief priests and the multitudes, "I find no basis for a charge against this man" (Luke 23:4). After Jesus returned from Herod's court, Pilate repeated to the chief priests and the rulers of the people, "I have examined [Jesus] in your presence and have found no basis for your charges against him" (verse 14). Pilate went on to say, "Neither has Herod, for he sent him back to us; as you can see, he has done nothing to deserve death" (verse 15). One final time Pilate asked the Jewish leaders, "Why? What crime has this man committed? I have found in him no grounds for the death penalty" (verse 22).

No, our Jesus committed no crime. He committed no sin.

Do you realize that, like Jesus, you can call upon God to help you make the right choices in life? You can experience victory over sin? You can make choices that say *no* to sin, choices that may require you to *do it, take it,* or *don't do it,* whatever the case may be? Scottish devotional writer Thomas Guthrie warned,

> Never fear to suffer; but oh! fear to sin. If you must choose between them, prefer the greatest suffering to the smallest sin.[1]

Can you make this the perspective of your heart too? When you turn to God for help, He will help you choose not to sin.

Jesus Spoke No Sin

Not only was Jesus sinless in deed, but He was also sinless in word. Peter tells us, "No deceit was found in his mouth" (1 Peter 2:22). Even after careful examination, Jesus' accusers found no craftiness or trickery.[2] Jesus always spoke the truth—100 percent of the time. He always spoke and acted with pure motives. Nothing of deceit or guile could be uncovered...because it just wasn't there!

And here's something else—Jesus didn't talk back. He refused to answer at His trial. When falsely accused by the chief priests and elders, "he gave no answer" (Matthew 27:12). When questioned by Pilate, Jesus "made no reply, not even to a single charge" (verse 14). When Caiaphas and the Sanhedrin challenged Him—"Are you not going to answer? What is this testimony that these men are bringing against you?" (Mark 14:60)—Jesus "remained silent and gave no answer" (verse 61). Instead of verbally pressing His case to people who did not have ears to hear, Jesus silently submitted to harsh treatment and a cruel death that He did not deserve.

Jesus Did Not Resist

Jesus also did not resist His accusers and enemies. He absolutely refused to fight verbally or physically. We read, for instance, that while being insulted, He did not retaliate (1 Peter 2:23). To be insulted or reviled means to be harshly cursed with a string of sharp, abusive words.[3] And that's the treatment our Jesus, the sinless Lamb of God, suffered!

What did Jesus do when He was attacked verbally and physically? The Bible says that "when he suffered, he made no threats" (1 Peter 2:23). Here, "suffered" means buffeted, struck with fists (Matthew 26:67). Peter is remembering the blows inflicted upon Jesus by the servants, the scorn of the high priest, the stripes, the cross...and the silent submission of Jesus. As one scholar explains, "Under sustained and repeated provocation, never once did [Jesus] break the silence. All the time during which He was physically beaten, He was not reviling back. All the time during which He was suffering, he was not resorting to threats."[4] Even "continuous suffering at the hands of the mob did not elicit from our Lord any retaliatory words."[5]

Of course sinful, scornful, harsh words wouldn't fit the picture of Jesus' perfect godliness! Reacting is something you and I might do...but not Jesus. When He was unfairly treated, He did not utter threats, condemn His oppressors, or call down judgment upon them. No, He kept His mouth closed. In the words of Isaiah, "He was oppressed and afflicted, yet he did not open his mouth; he was led like a lamb to the slaughter, and as a sheep before her shearers is silent, so he did not open his mouth" (Isaiah 53:7).

Oh, how precious is our Jesus! And oh, to be like Him! I'm sure your heart hurts as you think about this scene of horror and evil. The Savior's response is sobering. It should make you think (and purpose!) that surely...if He exhibited such graciousness—such faithfulness, gentleness, and self-control—in these evil circumstances, then you can do the same in your much quieter sphere of life and service. And surely...if He bore with tranquility the pain and suffering caused by His killers, you can quietly endure the ill treatment you receive from others. And surely...if He kept His mouth shut when He was innocent, you can do the same.

But by now you should also know that you can only do these things and give these responses by the power of God's Spirit. He is the one who fills you with His faithfulness, gentleness, and self-control. My dear traveling friend, don't fail to look to God for His help in being more like Jesus.

And now...a final prayer of thanksgiving...

> It is with overflowing hearts, O Father,
> That we whisper yet another "Thank You"—
> This time for the grace of Your Son
>> Who demonstrated complete faithfulness to You,
>> Who accepted in gentleness such unjust mis-
>>> treatment, and
>> Who exhibited self-control
>>> in the harshest of circumstances
> As He walked to the cross to die for us.
> May we receive Your grace...that we may
>> Faithfully do all that You ask of us,
>> Gently and quietly suffer what comes our
>>> way, and,
>> In control of ourselves, do nothing that
>>> dishonors Your worthy Name.
> In Jesus' name, our Model and Savior and Lord.
>> Amen.

Things to Do Today to Grow More Like Jesus

1. Reflect on your life—Pause and pray about your conduct or lifestyle as you consider your Savior and your call to follow His example. Do any glaring areas of sin leap to your mind and heart?

2. Confess any sin areas now—Follow up by determining what you will do to deal with them, eliminate them, to "don't do it!" Remember, "He who conceals his sins does not prosper, but whoever confesses and renounces them finds mercy" (Proverbs 28:13).

3. Rejoice that you have forgiveness in Jesus—"If we confess our sins, he is faithful and just and will forgive us our sins and purify us from all unrighteousness" (1 John 1:9).

Would You Like to Know More About Growing Like Jesus? Check It Out!

✓ Read 1 Peter 2:22. Note in the blank below the first of the two facts written about Jesus' conduct and behavior.

Jesus _____.

What do these scriptures relate about the truth of this fact?

Acts 3:13-15—

Hebrews 4:15—

Hebrews 7:26—

1 John 3:5—

✓ Read 1 Peter 2:22 again and note in the blank below the second of the two facts written about Jesus' conduct and behavior.

Jesus _____ .

What do these scriptures relate about the truth of this fact?

Isaiah 53:7—

Mark 14:60-61—

Mark 15:4-5—

Luke 23:8-9—

✓ Read 1 Peter 2:23 and note two additional facts written about Jesus' conduct and behavior.

First, Jesus _____ .

Second, Jesus _____

but _____ .

What do these scriptures relate about Jesus' treatment by His enemies?

Matthew 26:67-68—

Matthew 27:26—

Matthew 27:27-32—

Matthew 27:39-40—

Matthew 27:41-43—

Matthew 27:44—

What did Jesus do instead, according to Luke 23:34 and 46?

Getting the Most Out of Your Life

Whew! We made it! You and I have completed our walking tour of the fruit of the Spirit! Together we strolled along the path, moving from group to group, from fruit to fruit. With God's Word as our guide, we read about each grace—each fruit—what each one is and how it can be cultivated as we walk with God. I'm glad for the time we had to study, to enjoy each fruit. We've seen and tasted them all. And we now know more about bearing God's fruit in our lives.

As we leave these pages and one another, I want you to take God's message with you into your daily life. I want you (and me too!) to get your act together, get along with everybody, get the right attitudes, get it all going, and get the most out of your life. It's one thing to talk about spiritual fruit, but God wants you to live it out. He wants you to walk the walk! As you've seen, His Word describes exactly what He wants your life to look like and what He wants others to see in you as you bear the fruit of His Spirit in real, everyday life.

A Story

Let me tell you a story about someone who walked with God and lived out the fruit of the spirit...and its impact on a young woman. His name is Sam Britten. Sam was an elder and a servant at my former church. He was also the director of the Center of Activities of the Physically Disabled at California State University at Northridge. I have known Sam for decades, but one of the students on campus helped me appreciate him even more.

Judi had heard about the remarkable things going on in the center for the physically disabled, which was just down the hall from one of her classes. So one afternoon, out of curiosity, she entered the room and stood silently watching. What she saw was Dr. Britten, down on his knees, helping and encouraging one of his disabled students.

Judi, who was not a Christian but who had heard of Jesus, said: "As I stood there watching Dr. Britten and saw his love and kindness and patience and gentleness with that student, I thought, 'This must be what Jesus was like!'" Daily Judi was drawn to Dr. Britten's room. And again and again she saw this same scene. "Some days," she confessed, "I had to leave the room and go out into the hall so that I could weep. It was so moving to watch this man!"

Approaching Margie, one of Sam's assistants, Judi asked if she knew what made Sam like Jesus. Margie answered, "Oh, he's a Christian. He knows Jesus, and he reads his Bible a lot and prays. In fact, we all pray together every day before the people arrive for treatment." Well, you guessed it. Soon Judi had bought herself a Bible. She began reading it and praying. She also found a church, and within a year Judi had given her heart to Jesus.

Dear reader and friend, this picture of Sam Britten is what this book is all about—Jesus in you, Jesus visible to others as you walk by the Spirit, Jesus loving and serving others through you, Jesus on display in you just as He is displayed in Sam Britten. When you get it together spiritually and walk by the Spirit, you behave as Jesus did. Filled with His Holy Spirit, you can model Him to a needy world.

A Comment

The apostle John wrote about this kind of Christlikeness saying "When he appears, we shall be like him" (1 John 3:2). Then, in the next verse, he tells us how we can become like Jesus now: "Everyone who has this hope fixed in him purifies himself, just as he is pure" (verse 3). And how does this purification happen, and how can we help it happen?

To wrap up our precious walk with God through this book, read these comments by British preacher Dr. John Blanchard. He also gives us some steps we can take:

> Everyone who truly believes that he will one day be like Christ...surely purifies himself and relentlessly pursues godliness as a number one priority. This is the mark of the true child of God. We are to feast our eyes upon Christ, upon as much of Christ as we can find in the

sacred Scriptures. We are to do everything that we possibly can: We are to wrestle and fight and pray and be disciplined in order that more and more we become like Christ—whatever the cost—knowing that every sin that is overcome, every temptation that is resisted, every virtue that is gained is another step, another step, another step, another step toward that moment when we shall be like Him.

A Prayer

When Dr. Blanchard finished his sermon, he prayed the following prayer—a prayer for you and for me as we, God's women, seek to walk with God and model Jesus to a needy world. Make this prayer your own!

> We can bless You for all of Your goodness *to* us, for the enabling of the Holy Spirit *in* our lives, for every word of Scripture that has come to burn in our hearts, for every step of progress that has been made, for every victory that has been gained, for every temptation that has been resisted. And we can and do praise You as well, knowing that it is only by Your grace and power that these things were achieved.[1]

Becoming More Like Jesus

Look back through your book and write out the short slogan or motto for each fruit of the Spirit. Remembering, for instance, that "love is the sacrifice of self" will help you respond to the events of your day—and life—in a godly way, to be more like Jesus. Review this list often.

1. Love...

2. Joy...

3. Peace...

4. Patience...

5. Kindness...

6. Goodness...

7. Faithfulness...

8. Gentleness...

9. Self-control...

Notes

Chapter 1—Getting It All Going

1. Merrill E. Unger, *Unger's Bible Dictionary* (Chicago: Moody Press, 1972), p. 382.
2. Alfred Martin, *John, Life Through Believing* (Chicago: Moody Bible Institute, 1981), p. 92.
3. Everett F. Harrison, *John, The Gospel of Faith* (Chicago: Moody Press, 1962), p. 91.
4. William Barclay, *The Gospel of John,* vol. 2, rev. ed. (Philadelphia: The Westminster Press, 1975), p. 176.
5. Harrison, *John, The Gospel of Faith,* p. 91.
6. Albert M. Wells, Jr., ed., *Inspiring Quotations Contemporary & Classical* (Nashville: Thomas Nelson Publishers, 1988), p. 158.
7. Elizabeth George, *A Young Woman's Call to Prayer—Talking with God About Your Life* (Eugene, OR: Harvest House Publishers, 2005).
8. Charles Wesley, "And Can It Be that I Should Gain," *Psalms and Hymns* (1738.)

Chapter 2—A Loving Heart

1. William Barclay, *The Letters to the Galatians and Ephesians,* rev. ed. (Philadelphia: The Westminster Press, 1976), p. 50.
2. John MacArthur, Jr., *Liberty in Christ* (Panorama City, CA: Word of Grace Communications, 1986), p. 88.

Chapter 3—A Happy Heart

1. John MacArthur, Jr., *Liberty in Christ* (Panorama City, CA: Word of Grace Communications, 1986), p. 90.
2. William Barclay, *The Letters to the Galatians and Ephesians,* rev. ed. (Philadelphia: The Westminster Press, 1976), p. 50.
3. William Barclay, *The Letters of James and Peter,* rev. ed. (Philadelphia: The Westminster Press, 1976), p. 178.
4. H.D.M. Spence and Joseph S. Exell, eds., *The Pulpit Commentary,* vol. 22 (Grand Rapids, MI: William B. Eerdmans Publishing Company, 1978), p. 6.
5. W.H. Griffith Thomas, *The Apostle Peter* (Grand Rapids, MI: Kregel Publications, 1984), p. 162.
6. John MacArthur, Jr., *The MacArthur New Testament Commentary, Galatians* (Chicago: Moody Press, 1987), p. 166.
7. Herbert Lockyer, *All the Promises of the Bible* (Grand Rapids, MI: Zondervan Publishing House, 1962), p. 10.

Chapter 4—A Quiet Heart

1. Kenneth S. Wuest, *Wuest's Word Studies in the Greek New Testament,* vol. 1 (Grand Rapids, MI: William B. Eerdmans Publishing Company, 1973), p. 160.

2. William Barclay, *The Letters to the Galatians and Ephesians,* rev. ed. (Philadelphia: The Westminster Press, 1976), p. 50.
3. Howard F. Vos, *Galatians, A Call to Christian Liberty* (Chicago: Moody Press, 1971), p. 107.
4. Albert M. Wells, Jr., ed., *Inspiring Quotations Contemporary & Classical* (Nashville: Thomas Nelson Publishers, 1988), p. 152.

Chapter 5—Looking at Jesus' Attitudes

1. John MacArthur, Jr., *The MacArthur New Testament Commentary, Matthew 24–28* (Chicago: Moody Press, 1989), p. 167.
2. William Hendriksen, *New Testament Commentary, Matthew* (Grand Rapids, MI: Baker Book House, 1973), p. 917.

Chapter 6—A Time to Do Nothing

1. Charles F. Pfeiffer and Everett F. Harrison, eds., *The Wycliffe Bible Commentary* (Chicago: Moody Press, 1973), p. 1297.
2. Alan Cole, "The Epistle of Paul to the Galatians," *Tyndale New Testament Commentaries* (Grand Rapids, MI: William B. Eerdmans Publishing Company, 1965), p. 167.
3. John MacArthur, Jr., *The MacArthur New Testament Commentary, Galatians* (Chicago: Moody Press, 1987), p. 167.
4. Howard F. Vos, *Galatians, A Call to Christian Liberty* (Chicago: Moody Press, 1971), p. 108.
5. Merrill F. Unger, *Unger's Bible Dictionary* (Chicago: Moody Press, 1972), p. 829.
6. George Sweeting, *Love Is the Greatest* (Chicago: Moody Press, 1974), p. 53.
7. John MacArthur, Jr., *Liberty in Christ* (Panorama City, CA: Word of Grace Communications, 1986), p. 92.
8. H.D.M. Spence and Joseph S. Exell, eds., *The Pulpit Commentary,* vol. 20 (Grand Rapids, MI: William B. Eerdmans Publishing Company, 1978), p. 287.
9. William Barclay, *The Letters to the Galatians and Ephesians,* rev. ed. (Philadelphia: The Westminster Press, 1976), p. 51.
10. Ibid., p. 51.
11. D.L. Moody, *Notes from My Bible and Thoughts from My Library* (Grand Rapids, MI: Baker Book House, 1979), p. 323.
12. Spence and Exell, eds., *The Pulpit Commentary,* vol. 20, p. 294.

Chapter 7—A Time to Do Something

1. William Barclay, *The Letters to the Galatians and Ephesians,* rev. ed. (Philadelphia: The Westminster Press, 1976), p. 158.
2. John MacArthur, Jr., *The MacArthur New Testament Commentary, Colossians and Philemon* (Chicago: Moody Press, 1992), p. 155.
3. John M. Drescher, *Spirit Fruit* (Scottdale, PA: Herald Press, 1974), p. 210.
4. Ibid., p. 206.
5. Anne Ortlund, *Disciplines of the Beautiful Woman* (Waco, TX: Word, Inc., 1977), pp. 96, 98.

6. Alan Cole, "The Epistle of Paul to the Galatians," *Tyndale New Testament Commentaries* (Grand Rapids, MI: William B. Eerdmans Publishing Company, 1965), p 167.

Chapter 8—A Time to Do Everything

1. John W. Cowart, *People Whose Faith Got Them into Trouble* (Downers Grove, IL: InterVarsity Press, 1990).
2. Ibid., pp. 13-14.
3. Merrill F. Unger, *Unger's Bible Dictionary* (Chicago: Moody Press, 1972), p. 420.
4. John MacArthur, Jr., *The MacArthur New Testament Commentary, Galatians* (Chicago: Moody Press, 1987), p. 168.
5. Kenneth S. Wuest, *Word Studies in the Greek New Testament,* vol. 1 (Grand Rapids, MI: William B. Eerdmans Publishing Company, 1974), p. 160.
6. Howard F. Vos, *Galatians, A Call to Christian Liberty* (Chicago: Moody Press, 1973), p. 108.
7. William Hendriksen, *Exposition of the Pastoral Epistles, New Testament Commentary* (Grand Rapids, MI: Baker Book House, 1976), p. 188.
8. Ibid., p. 107.
9. William Hendriksen, *Exposition of the Bible According to Luke, New Testament Commentary* (Grand Rapids, MI: Baker Book House, 1978), p. 558.
10. Oswald Chambers, *Studies in the Sermon on the Mount* (Fort Washington, PA: Christian Literature Crusade, 1960), p. 53.
11. Albert M. Wells, Jr., ed., *Inspiring Quotations Contemporary & Classical* (Nashville: Thomas Nelson Publishers, 1988), p. 82.
12. Neil S. Wilson, ed., *The Handbook of Bible Application* (Wheaton, IL: Tyndale House Publishers, Inc., 1992), p. 369.
13. Dan Baumann, *Extraordinary Living for Ordinary People* (Irvine, CA: Harvest House Publishers, 1978), pp. 83-84.

Chapter 9—Looking at Jesus' Actions

1. William Hendriksen, *Exposition of the Gospel According to Luke, New Testament Commentary* (Grand Rapids, MI: Baker Book House, 1978), p. 989.

Chapter 10—A Choice to Just Do It

1. Albert M. Wells, Jr., ed., *Inspiring Quotations Contemporary & Classical* (Nashville: Thomas Nelson Publishers, 1988), p. 69.
2. H.D.M. Spence and Joseph S. Exell, eds., *The pulpit Commentary,* vol. 20 (Grand Rapids, MI: William B. Eerdmans Publishing Co., 1978), p. 287.
3. John MacArthur, Jr., *The MacArthur New Testament Commentary, Galatians* (Chicago: Moody Press, 1987), p. 169.
4. Richard Shelley Taylor, *The Disciplined Life* (Minneapolis: Dimension Books, Bethany Fellowship, Inc., 1962), p. 37.
5. Vanita Hampton and Carol Plueddemann, eds., *World Shapers* (Wheaton, IL: Harold Shaw Publishers, 1991), p. 17.

6. Richard C. Halverson, "Perspective" newsletter, 10/26/77.

Chapter 11—A Choice to Take It

1. William Hendriksen, *Exposition of the Gospel According to Matthew, New Testament Commentary* (Grand Rapids, MI: Baker Book House, 1975), pp. 271-72.
2. William Barclay, *The Letters to the Galatians and Ephesians,* rev. ed. (Philadelphia: The Westminster Press, 1976), p. 52.
3. *Webster's New Dictionary of Synonyms* (Springfield, MA: G. & C. Merriam Company, Publishers, 1973), p. 812.
4. Merrill F. Unger, *Unger's Bible Dictionary* (Chicago: Moody Press, 1972), p. 709.
5. 1 Peter 2:13.
6. 1 Peter 2:18.
7. 1 Peter 2:21-25.
8. 1 Peter 3:1.
9. Robert Jamieson, A.R. Fausset, and David Brown, *Commentary on the Whole Bible* (Grand Rapids, MI: Zondervan Publishing House, 1973), p. 1475.
10. Kenneth S. Wuest, *Wuest's Word Studies from the Greek New Testament,* vol. 2 (Grand Rapids, MI: William B. Eerdmans Publishing Company, 1974), p. 81.
11. Albert M. Wells, Jr., ed., *Inspiring Quotations Contemporary & Classical* (Nashville: Thomas Nelson Publishers, 1988), p. 92.
12. W.E. Vine, *An Expository Dictionary of New Testament Words* (Old Tappan, NJ: Fleming H. Revell Company, 1966), pp. 55-56.
13. Ibid., p. 56.
14. Don Baker, *Pain's Hidden Purpose* (Portland, OR: Multnomah Press, 1984), pp. 86-89.

Chapter 12—A Choice to Not Do It

1. J. Oswald Sanders, *Spiritual Leadership,* rev. ed. (Chicago: Moody Press, 1980), pp. 71-72.
2. Robert Jamieson, A.R. Fausset, and David Brown, *Commentary of the Whole Bible* (Grand Rapids, MI: Zondervan Publishing House, 1973), p. 1275.
3. William Barclay, *The Letters to the Galatians and Ephesians,* rev. ed. (Philadelphia: The Westminster Press, 1976), p. 52.
4. W.E. Vine, *An Expository Dictionary of New Testament Words* (Old Tappan, NJ: Fleming H. Revell Company, 1966), p. 114.
5. Charles F. Pfeiffer and Everett F. Harrison, *The Wycliffe Bible Commentary* (Chicago: Moody Press, 1973), p. 1297.
6. John MacArthur, Jr., *Liberty in Christ* (Panorama City, CA: Word of Grace Communities, 1986), p. 96.
7. H.D.M. Spence and Joseph S. Exell, eds., *The Pulpit Commentary,* vol. 20 (Grand Rapids, MI: William B. Eerdmans Publishing Company, 1978), p. 287.

8. Kenneth S. Wuest, *Wuest's Word Studies from the Greek New Testament* (Grand Rapids, MI: William B. Eerdmans Publishing Company, 1974), p. 160.

9. Dan Baumann, *Extraordinary Living for Ordinary People* (Irvine, CA: Harvest House Publishers, 1978), pp. 118-19.

10. Bruce Wideman, *Presbyterian Journal,* July 30, 1975, p. 7.

11. Quoted in Luis Palau, *Heart After God* (Portland, OR: Multnomah Press, 1978), p. 70.

12. John H. Timmerman, *The Way of Christian Living* (Grand Rapids, MI: William B. Eerdmans Publishing Company, 1987), pp. 147-48.

Chapter 13—Looking at Jesus

1. D.L. Moody, *Notes from My Bible and Thoughts from My Library* (Grand Rapids, MI: Baker Book House, 1979), p. 362.

2. Kenneth S. Wuest, *Wuest's Word Studies from the Greek New Testament,* vol. 2 (Grand Rapids, MI: William B. Eerdmans Publishing Company, 1973), p. 67.

3. Ibid., pp. 67-68.

4. Alan M. Stibbs, *The First Epistle General of Peter, The Tyndale New Testament Commentaries* (Grand Rapids, MI: William B. Eerdmans Publishing Company, 1976), p. 118.

5. Wuest, *Wuest's Word Studies*, pp. 67-68.

Getting the Most Out of Your Life

1. John Blanchard, "The Most Amazing Statement in Scripture" (Grace to You, P.O. Box 4000, Panorama City, CA 91412).

Personal Notes

Personal Notes

_____

_____

_____

_____

_____

_____

_____

_____

_____

_____

_____

_____

_____

_____

_____

_____

_____

Personal Notes

Personal Notes

Personal Notes

_____

_____

_____

_____

_____

_____

_____

_____

_____

_____

_____

_____

_____

_____

_____

_____

_____

_____

A Young Woman After God's Own Heart

Discover God's plan and purpose
for your life!

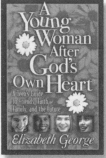

What does it mean to pursue God's heart in your everyday life? It means understanding and following God's perfect plan for your friendships, your faith, your family relationships, and your future. Bible teacher Elizabeth George reveals how you can...

- grow closer to God

- enjoy meaningful relationships

- make wise choices

- become spiritually strong

- build a better future

- fulfill the desires of your heart.

Get caught up in the exciting adventure of a lifetime—become a woman after God's own heart!

A Young Woman's Call to Prayer

God wants to hear from you!

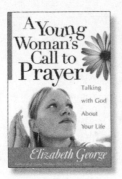

God has given you an amazing gift—the ability to personally talk with Him every day! Through prayer, you can share with God your joys and triumphs, hurts and fears, and wants and needs, knowing that He cares about every detail of your life. Bestselling author Elizabeth George will help you...

- develop a stronger relationship with God

- set a regular time to talk to Him

- share sticky situations and special concerns with Him

- discover and live His will

- worship Him daily

God is your forever friend—and He's always ready to talk with you! Experience the joy of knowing Him in a very real way as you develop an active, personal, and powerful prayer life!

A Young Man
After God's Own Heart

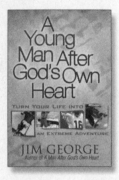

Get ready to experience the adventure of a lifetime!

Pursuing God really is an adventure—one that can sometimes get extreme. Becoming a young man after God's own heart is a lot like climbing a mountain. You'll find all kinds of challenges on the way up!

But the awesome view at the top is well worth the trip. As you go higher and higher, you'll experience the thrill of knowing real success in life—the kind that counts with God. And it all starts by learning God's priorities for you, including...

- building your faith

- Choosing the right kinds of friends

- Getting along at home

- Making wise choices about the future

- Fighting the battle against temptation

Once you get started on the journey, you'll never be the same

BIBLE STUDIES *for* BUSY WOMEN

A WOMAN AFTER GOD'S OWN HEART® BIBLE STUDIES

*E*lizabeth takes women step-by-step through the Scriptures, sharing wisdom she's gleaned from more than 30 years as a women's Bible teacher.

Character Studies

Old Testament Studies

New Testament Studies

NEW

Understanding Your Blessings in Christ

EPHESIANS

Elizabeth George

Books by Elizabeth George

- Beautiful in God's Eyes
- Finding God's Path Through Your Trials
- Following God with All Your Heart
- Life Management for Busy Women
- Loving God with All Your Mind
- A Mom After God's Own Heart
- Powerful Promises for Every Woman
- The Remarkable Women of the Bible
- Small Changes for a Better Life
- Walking with the Women of the Bible
- A Wife After God's Own Heart
- A Woman After God's Own Heart®
- A Woman After God's Own Heart® Deluxe Edition
- A Woman After God's Own Heart®—A Daily Devotional
- A Woman After God's Own Heart® Collection
- A Woman's Call to Prayer
- A Woman's High Calling
- A Woman's Walk with God
- A Young Woman After God's Own Heart
- A Young Woman After God's Own Heart—A Devotional
- A Young Woman's Call to Prayer
- A Young Woman's Walk with God

Study Guides

- Beautiful in God's Eyes Growth & Study Guide
- Finding God's Path Through Your Trials Growth & Study Guide
- Following God with All Your Heart Growth & Study Guide
- Life Management for Busy Women Growth & Study Guide
- Loving God with All Your Mind Growth & Study Guide
- A Mom After God's Own Heart Growth & Study Guide
- The Remarkable Women of the Bible Growth & Study Guide
- Small Changes for a Better Life Growth & Study Guide
- Understanding Your Blessings in Christ
- A Wife After God's Own Heart Growth & Study Guide
- A Woman After God's Own Heart® Growth & Study Guide
- A Woman's Call to Prayer Growth & Study Guide
- A Woman's High Calling Growth & Study Guide
- A Woman's Walk with God Growth & Study Guide

Children's Books

- God's Wisdom for Little Girls
- A Little Girl After God's Own Heart

Books by Jim & Elizabeth George

- God Loves His Precious Children
- God's Wisdom for Little Boys
- A Little Boy After God's Own Heart

Books by Jim George

- The Bare Bones Bible® Handbook
- The Bare Bones Bible® Bios
- A Husband After God's Own Heart
- A Man After God's Own Heart
- The Remarkable Prayers of the Bible
- A Young Man After God's Own Heart